Abraham Lincoln

TIME

MANAGING EDITOR Richard Stengel
DEPUTY MANAGING EDITOR Adi Ignatius
ART DIRECTOR Arthur Hochstein

Abraham Lincoln An Illustrated History of His Life and Times

EDITOR Kelly Knauer
DESIGNER Ellen Fanning
PICTURE EDITOR Patricia Cadley
WRITER/RESEARCHER Matthew McCann Fenton
COPY EDITOR Bruce Christopher Carr

TIME INC. HOME ENTERTAINMENT

PUBLISHER Richard Fraiman
GENERAL MANAGER Steven Sandonato
EXECUTIVE DIRECTOR, MARKETING SERVICES Carol Pittard
DIRECTOR, RETAIL & SPECIAL SALES Tom Mifsud
DIRECTOR, NEW PRODUCT DEVELOPMENT Peter Harper
ASSISTANT DIRECTOR, NEWSSTAND MARKETING Laura Adam
ASSISTANT DIRECTOR, BRAND MARKETING Joy Butts
ASSOCIATE COUNSEL Helen Wan
SENIOR BRAND MANAGER, TWRS/M Holly Oakes
BOOK PRODUCTION MANAGER Suzanne Janso
DESIGN & PREPRESS MANAGER Anne-Michelle Gallero
ASSOCIATE BRAND MANAGER Michela Wilde
ASSISTANT PREPRESS MANAGER Alex Voznesenskiy

SPECIAL THANKS TO:
Glenn Buonocore, Susan Chodakiewicz, Margaret Hess, Brynn Joyce, Robert Marasco, Brooke Reger, Mary Sarro-Waite, Ilene Schreider, Adriana Tierno

FOR ASSISTANCE WITH PICTURE RESEARCH, THE EDITORS WISH TO THANK:
James Cornelius, Jennifer Ericson and Roberta Fairburn of The Abraham Lincoln Presidential Library; Michelle Ganz of the Abraham Lincoln Library and Museum at Abraham Lincoln Memorial University; Bertha Schmalfeldt of the Abraham Lincoln Birthplace National Historic Site; Candy Knox of Lincoln's New Salem State Historic Site; Mike Capps at the Lincoln Boyhood National Memorial; Erin A.C. Mast of President Lincoln's Cottage National Trust Historic Site; Keya Morgan of Keya Morgan Gallery & Lincolnimages.com

ISBN 10: 1-60320-063-0 • ISBN 13: 978-1-60320-063-9 • Library of Congress number: 2008909717
TIME Books is a trademark of Time Inc.

We welcome your comments and suggestions about TIME Books. Please write to us at:
TIME Books • Attention: Book Editors • PO Box 11016 • Des Moines, IA 50336-1016

If you would like to order any of our hardcover Collector's Edition books, please call us at 1-800-327-6388
(Monday through Friday, 7 a.m.–8 p.m., or Saturday, 7 a.m.–6 p.m., Central time).

PRINTED IN THE UNITED STATES OF AMERICA

To read more of TIME's coverage of Abraham Lincoln and other U.S. Presidents, visit: **Time.com**

Almost larger than life *Visiting the battlefield at Sharpsburg, Md., in October 1862 after the costly Union victory near Antietam Creek, the 16th President towers over security man Allan Pinkerton and General John A. McClernand*

Contents

Work in progress *Like the Union it represented, the U.S. Capitol
building remained incomplete during Lincoln's presidency, as it
awaited construction of its crowning dome*

HULTON DEUTSCH COLLECTION—CORBIS

Fanfare for a Common Man

Abraham Lincoln is the archetypal American, because his
extraordinary moral compass revolved around an ordinary life

H E IS THE GREATEST, THE CLASSIC, THE ARCHETYPI-
cal individual in the American imagination.
Perhaps that's because Abraham Lincoln embod-
ied a notable American type: the common man who is
yet uncommon. The common stamp was indelible on
him, whether he was campaigning in Sangamon
County, wearing a calico shirt and old straw hat, with
6 in. of blue socks showing from beneath his pants, or
whether he stood at a White House reception, his hands
enormous in white gloves that as often as not burst
under some diplomat's hand clasp. And yet Lincoln
always had a sense of being different and apart. John
Hay, his longtime presidential secretary, wrote that it
was "absurd to call him a modest man."

Innumerable times Lincoln could have settled for
what he had. He could have stayed a ferryman on the
Ohio River, where as a boy he was overwhelmed by
earning $2 in one day. He could have taken up the
indolent hunting, fishing and Shakespeare-quoting life
of his mentor Jack Kelso in New Salem, Ill. He could
have remained postmaster or storekeeper or a circuit-
riding lawyer, instead of running for office. But for all
his unassuming qualities, he had a sense of destiny.
When he was 28 he spoke at the Young Men's Lyceum of
Springfield and sounded an early note of personal
longing: "Towering genius disdains a beaten path," he
said. "It seeks regions hitherto unexplored ..."

The Illinois statehouse at Vandalia, where Lincoln first
served as a legislator, boasted a Greek-columned portico,
and this was not inappropriate, for the grass-roots democracy of the period constituted a kind of prairie Athens
in which legislators were not remote and impersonal
but known to all the voters and directly involved
in their concerns. In that school he learned to be a
politician first and last—and to respect organization.

During the 1860 Republican convention at the Chicago
Wigwam, his supporters put through his nomination by
crass maneuvering and packing the galleries with Lincoln men. Deals were offered right and left, and Lincoln
honored them later. But he always knew when to draw
the line. At the height of the Civil War, when allies urged
him to cut the draft to win popularity, he refused, saying,
"What is the presidency to me if I have no country?"

Caught between extreme Abolitionists and extreme
Southerners, Lincoln held firmly to the center. Again
and again he defined his lonely position between the
poles. When John Brown was executed, he told Northerners that since Brown had acted lawlessly, they had no
right to object. But he told Southerners that if they
should try to destroy the Union, "it will be our duty to
deal with you as old John Brown has been dealt with."

The complexities of his task were defined by his
biographer Benjamin P. Thomas: "To hold together in
wartime a party made up of Abolitionists and Negro-
haters, high- and low-tariff men, hard- and soft-money
men, former Whigs and erstwhile Democrats, prohibi-
tionists and German beer-drinkers, Know-Nothings and
immigrants."

Lincoln had no administrative experience when he
became President, and his military experience consisted
of a captaincy in the Black Hawk War, in which he admitted to never having seen any "live, fighting Indians."
And yet he proved himself a sound strategist, against
the enemy as well as against his own generals. He
suffered through the hesitations of General George Mc-
Clellan, complaining that sending him reinforcements
was like shoving fleas across a barnyard—so few of
them seemed to get there. Later, he turned to Joe Hooker.
There had been rumors that a clique, including Hooker,
wanted to set up a military dictatorship. Lincoln flung
him a magnificent challenge: "Only those generals who
gain successes can set up dictators. What I now ask of
you is military success, and I will risk the dictatorship."

He made mistakes. He was vilified both for being too
soft and for being too hard. He was called a tyrant for
suspending habeas corpus and imprisoning dissidents.
His answer: "I expect to maintain this contest until
successful, or till I die, or am conquered, or my term
expires, or Congress or the country forsake me."

Beyond the triumphs of his leadership, he retained a
special genius—not of strategy, not even of politics—
the genius of being a person. He was the gaunt figure

*This unsigned essay was first published, in substantially different
form, in* TIME's *40th-anniversary issue in 1963, the centennial
year of Lincoln's Gettysburg Address*

walking alone at night to the War Department telegraph office to read late dispatches or wandering about the White House in his short nightshirt ("setting out behind," said Hay, "like the tailfeathers of an enormous ostrich") to read a funny story to his secretaries.

Yet this awkward, morose President carried out one of the most dramatic acts of human liberation in history. Lincoln was certain that both emancipation and the Union served universal causes. He said, "In giving freedom to the slave, we assure freedom to the free." In his mind, the American cause was "to elevate the condition of men, to lift artificial weights from all shoulders, to clear the paths of laudable pursuit for all."

And so, out of large and small facts of his life grew a man whom it is difficult to call a genius, and even more difficult to call anything less; a man who is beyond question a hero, and yet is so unheroic in appearance that he looks downright uneasy in stone. ■

The True Lincoln

He was underestimated as President, then turned into an
icon at his death. **Joshua Wolf Shenk** explores the personal
and political depth of the leader who saved the nation

W E DON'T OUTRIGHT INVENT HISTORY, BUT OFTEN
it is made by the questions we ask. Few figures
have provoked more questions than Abraham
Lincoln, both because of his broad importance and his
fantastic complexity. And few figures have proved so
malleable. At times, the bearded man in the stovepipe hat
seems much like a hologram, a medium for our fears and
fantasies. Recent claims that Lincoln was gay—based on
a tortured misreading of conventional 19th century sleep-
ing arrangements—resemble the long-standing efforts to
draft the famously nonsectarian man for one Christian denomination or another. Over the years, America's 16th
president has been trotted out to support everything
from communism and feminism to prohibitionism and
vegetarianism. But if a figure can be made to stand for
everything, does he really mean anything?

In 2009, as we celebrate the bicentennial of Lincoln's
birth and a trove of Lincoln scholarship has become instantly available on the Internet, primary material has become newly accessible and there's a renewed drive to get
him right. "We really are in a renaissance of Lincoln literature," notes Harold Holzer, a co-chairman of the Abraham Lincoln Bicentennial Commission. "All of the classic
works are being updated and improved upon. All the great
themes that hitherto we thought had been dealt with de-
finitively are being re-explored." In popular culture too,
there is a Lincoln boom: in 2005 a $150 million Lincoln li-
brary and museum complex opened in Springfield, Ill.
Barack Obama read Lincoln's works and historian Doris
Kearns Goodwin's study of Lincoln's Cabinet, *Team of Rivals*, as he assembled the team for his Administration.

But after 143 years of manipulation, can Lincoln's memory ever again find its true shape?

Abraham Lincoln died shortly after 7 a.m. on April 15,
1865. "Now he belongs to the ages," Edwin Stanton, Lincoln's Secretary of War, said at the President's deathbed. It

was a prescient thought, because it suggested not only
the long cultural presence ahead for Lincoln but also the
fact that generations would possess him.

From the start, his memory was molded to serve a purpose. When telegraph wires clicked with the news that
Lincoln had been shot at Ford's Theatre, the nation was facing the monumental and confounding task of restoring
peace after four years of broiling war. Lincoln had thought
both North and South were complicit in the shame of slavery. He even suggested, in his second Inaugural Address,
that God may have brought "this terrible war" to punish
both regions, urging the nation to bind up its wounds
"with malice towards none, with charity for all."

He wanted reconciliation, but his eulogists struck a different note. With a sentimental tip of the hat to the fallen
leader, many Northern journalists, preachers and politicians actually tried to use Lincoln's death to stoke the
fires of vengeance. "If the rebels can do a deed like this to
the kind, good, generous, tender-hearted ruler, whose
every thought was purity," exclaimed Benjamin Butler, a
general in the war, to a crowd in New York City, "whose
every desire a yearning for forgiveness and peace, what
shall be done to them in high places who guided the assassin's knife?" The crowd began to chant, "Hang them!
Hang them!" The assassination, Northern leaders saw,
had a great political value. "His death," noted a caucus of
Republican Congressmen, "is a godsend to our cause."

If his contemporaries quickly contradicted his ideas,
they were also slow to elevate him as an icon, even
though he had all the ingredients to be one: an epic time
(the split of a nation and a war over its future), bold ideas
(union and liberty) and a violent death. One reason is that
while people felt strongly the symbolic loss of a President

Joshua Wolf Shenk is the author of the acclaimed 2005 bestseller,
Lincoln's Melancholy

3

Lincoln has been trotted out to support everything from communism to prohibitionism

through the nation's first assassination, few knew what to make of Lincoln as a man. Beneath the spectacular symbols of mourning—houses draped in black, endless ceremonies as his body was taken by train from Washington to his home of Springfield—was an intense ambiguity: stories circulated regularly about him as a religious doubter, a teller of vulgar stories, an uncouth and awkward man, a usurper of power. But Republicans saw him as a great asset and tried to build a myth that would last—and do the party lasting good. In May 1865, the Republican editor Josiah Holland interviewed the President's law partner William Herndon at length. When the subject of religion came up, Herndon told him, "The less said, the better," unsure that the pious Holland would want the details of Lincoln's unorthodox history. How, for example, Lincoln had doubted the divinity of Christ and the infallibility of the Bible. "Oh, never mind," Holland said. "I'll fix that"—and his book made Lincoln a model Christian.

Holland wasn't alone in trying to "fix" Lincoln. "Those who have spoken most confidently of their knowledge of his personal qualities," Pennsylvania Republican Alexander McClure said of Lincoln, "are, as a rule, those who saw least of them below the surface." And many real Lincoln intimates kept a low profile, wishing to avoid the media circus. Meanwhile, one man who tried to talk about Lincoln in a complex and honest way paid a heavy price. After Lincoln died, Herndon solicited memories from men and women who had known him, identifying and tracking down crucial sources, then hounding them until they gave a statement or an interview. We call that kind of material oral history, but in the late 19th century it was just as likely to be called gossip—or, worse, scurrilous trash. Herndon thought that history should tell the full truth about a man and that Lincoln's character could only be magnified by a full portrait of it. He dug hard on matters that polite people thought should be left to rest: that Lincoln's mother had been born out of wedlock, for example, and that Lincoln as a young man had serious, nearly fatal depressions. Down on his luck, Herndon didn't publish his book until 1889. It didn't reach many readers, but he caught plenty of flak. "It vilely distorts the image of an ideal statesman, patriot, and martyr," the Chicago *Journal* said of his book. "It clothes him in vulgarity and grossness. Its indecencies are spread like a curtain to hide the colossal proportions and the splendid purity of his character."

The *Journal*, it's important to note, was a Republican paper. Today, when Lincoln is the favorite of everyone from George W. Bush to Mario Cuomo (not to mention Fidel Castro), it is easy to forget how partisan his memory once was.

In the late 19th century, a kind of cult of Lincoln grew up among the party faithful, with banquets on his birthday as a rite, while Southerners licked their wounds and Democrats rebuilt an organization that had been split in the war.

But in the early 20th century, Lincoln's appeal broadened considerably. By then, adults who had lived and suffered through the Civil War had died. Once a symbol of division, Lincoln came to be seen as a symbol of national peacemaking, admired alike by New York bankers and the Sons of the Confederate Veterans. In 1922, the Lincoln Memorial was dedicated, its structure modeled after the temples of ancient Greece, its statue reminiscent of Zeus on his throne, its location chosen to maximize the power of impression by an object of reverence and honor. In Illinois, sites associated with the 16th President were marked as "Lincoln shrines."

And so the legend grew. In the 1930s, Henry Fonda played Lincoln on the big screen and stonecutters carved his face on Mount Rushmore; in the 1940s, Aaron Copland's magisterial *Lincoln Portrait* debuted; in the1950s, Carl Sandburg held a joint session of Congress rapt with his speech that began, "Not often in the story of mankind does a man arrive on earth who is both steel and velvet, who is hard as rock and soft as a drifting fog, who holds in his heart and mind the paradox of terrible storm and peace unspeakable and perfect." In 1963, TIME put Lincoln on the cover of its 40th-anniversary issue, "The Individual in America," and christened him the embodiment of that quality "in the special double sense that Americans attributed to the word—the common man who is yet uncommon."

In retrospect, one of the high points of the Lincoln legend may also have marked its breaking point. In August 1963, the March on Washington for Jobs and Freedom gathered in front of the Lincoln Memorial, and the Rev. Martin Luther King Jr. began his landmark "I Have a Dream" speech by paying homage to Lincoln: "Five score years ago, a great American, in whose symbolic shadow we stand signed the Emancipation Proclamation. This momentous decree came as a great beacon of light of hope to millions of Negro slaves who had been seared in the flames of withering injustice. It came as a joyous daybreak to end the long night of captivity."

For decades, African Americans had not only remembered Lincoln kindly but also invoked him as a present-day force. "The rise of Jim Crow segregation in the South," explains historian Allen C. Guelzo, "occurred hand in hand

Rock star *Lincoln's visage is carved, far larger than life, into the face of Mount Rushmore in South Dakota in 1938*

with the efforts of Southerners to downplay the significance of slavery both for the war and for Lincoln, and blacks battled back by keeping slavery and Lincoln's image as the Great Emancipator at the forefront of the nation's memory." A common folktale in the mid-20th century South—which Leadbelly poignantly rendered in a song he recorded in the early 1940s—had Lincoln rising from the dead, coming down and bringing justice to the Jim Crow South.

But as the civil rights movement shone a spotlight on inequality and discrimination, Lincoln's image came in for a beating. The myth of Lincoln as the black man's best friend was hard to square with his own words, from the Lincoln-Douglas debates, that he had "no purpose to introduce political and social equality between the white and the black races" and that "there is a physical difference between the two, which in my judgment, will probably forever forbid their living upon the footing of perfect

Feet of clay *After the 1963 March on Washington, African Americans who as a people had idolized Lincoln for a century, began to discover that he was not a believer in racial equality*

equality." In a 1968 piece for *Ebony*, "Was Abe Lincoln a White Supremacist?", Lerone Bennett Jr. presented a Lincoln who often told racist jokes and who, well into his presidency, urged that freed blacks should leave the U.S. for another continent. Three decades later, Bennett returned to the theme in his book *Forced into Glory*, which became a best seller in black-interest bookstores.

Bennett's book is only one side of an ongoing argument over Lincoln and race, but its success served as a sharp reminder that, just as in all previous times, modern America will insist on seeing Lincoln on its own terms. Consider C.A. Tripp and his contention that Lincoln was gay. His

2005 book, *The Intimate World of Abraham Lincoln*, begins with the fact that Lincoln during his late 20s and early 30s shared a bed with a young man named Joshua Speed. As President, Lincoln may also have shared his bed with a captain of his guard unit in Washington.

But for men to share beds in the mid-19th century was as common and as mundane as men sharing houses or apartments in the early 21st. Tripp's claim proceeds from what Jonathan Ned Katz calls "epistemological hubris and ontological chutzpah." A scholar of 19th century sexuality, Katz explains that the terms homosexual and heterosexual did not exist in Lincoln's time, and that fact is just one piece of evidence that the concepts of gender, sexuality and same-sex relationships were radically different in Lincoln's world. In those days, men could be openly affectionate with one another, physically and verbally, without having to stake their identity on it.

So what do we, today, make of a world that operated according to such fundamentally different rules? And what do we make of the personal life of a leader so long encrusted in mythology? Fortunately, we've never been in a better position to see him. Along with fresh interest in the private lives of public figures, new trends in scholarship allow us a fresh chance to see Lincoln as he lived, thought and acted. Following the boom in oral history in the 1960s, today's Lincoln scholars are closely studying the massive body of recollections from people who knew him well, including intimate portraits that had long been neglected or obscured. In the past decade, more than a dozen volumes of essential primary evidence on Lincoln have been published, including original writings and research by his White House secretaries, John Hay and John Nicolay, and the Civil War dispatches of Lincoln intimate Noah Brooks. The granddaddy of all oral histories, the interviews and statements collected by Lincoln's law partner Herndon, are now easily available for the first time.

Then there's the Internet. It is possible to word-search, online, Lincoln's collected speeches, his known activities on each day of his life, his incoming correspondence and other ephemera at the Library of Congress and a vast array of primary sources from the 19th century, including letters, diaries and memoirs.

Those new historical tools can be easily abused, allowing writers with a fixed idea to go fish out evidence to support their claim. To do his research, Tripp took 80-some volumes of crucial Lincoln material, shipped them off to India to be digitized and put the results into a database. Then he did his research the new-fashioned way, by typing terms in a search bar. Presumably, a search for various body parts yielded the delicious bit that Lincoln's New Salem, Ill., friend William Greene considered his thighs "as perfect as a human being's could be."

But the revival of attention to primary sources has also peeled back the layers on Lincoln and produced a fresh round of portraits of his life and times. Douglas L. Wilson's incisive 1998 study, *In Honor's Voice*, cuts straight to Lincoln as a young man, showing him as creative and vulnerable, at once vastly ambitious and preoccupied with doubts and concerns about his future. Similarly, Guelzo's 1999 intellectual biography, *Abraham Lincoln: Redeemer President*, shows a man wrestling with the basic issues of fate and free will, torn between the Calvinism of his youth and the Enlightenment doctrines of freedom. Michael Burlingame's 2008 multivolume biography adds a tall stack of new documents to the record, including hundreds of newspaper articles that, Burlingame has determined, Lincoln wrote anonymously in his early political career. The articles shed new light on Lincoln's early political hackwork—which, Burlingame argues, makes his later achievements all the more remarkable.

My own research on Lincoln began in 1998, when I learned, much to my surprise, that the vital subject of his melancholy—which his friends uniformly identified as one of his chief characteristics—had been neglected for much of the 20th century. As I dug into the story, I learned about the two times, at ages 26 and 32, when Lincoln broke down so severely that he came near suicide; about his profound gloom in his middle years and his deliberate work to cope with it; and, finally, about how his depression both plagued him and fueled his great work as President. How could such an amazing story be so long left untold?

One answer to that question is a paradox about history. In order to appreciate Lincoln's significance for our time, we have to humble ourselves to an understanding of his time and how he lived. Previous works on Lincoln's psychology have tried to force his melancholy into the mold of psychoanalytic theory: finding explanations in his early childhood and searching his adult writings for clues about his lust for his mother and rage toward his father. But Lincoln had his own ideas about why he suffered. He was steeped in his own rich culture, in which psychology was wrapped up with philosophy and spirituality. By studying that context, alongside Lincoln's words and the commentaries of his friends, neighbors and colleagues, we can begin to see his story. When Lincoln wrote, "I am now the most miserable man living"; when he averred that melancholy is a "misfortune, not a fault"; and when he said that without his jokes, he would die, for they "are the vents of my moods & gloom," he was leaving a record, not only of how he lived and grew but also of how he saw the world.

Looking at how Lincoln really lived isn't always easy, but it has the chance to reinvigorate our relationship to a man that is otherwise threatened by so much iconography. And there's good reason to take Lincoln seriously: he offers many lessons for our own future. As we stand divided on religion, we can learn from a deeply spiritual man who was also highly skeptical of religious dogma, who felt guided by a divine will but insisted that every public act be justified in secular language and reason. As we stand divided over a war, we can learn from a man who insisted that conflict in arms raised questions about who we are as a people—and who understood that "right makes might."

There is something useful, too, in Lincoln's humor. At a time when we both take ourselves desperately seriously and scoff off all attempts at meaning, we can learn something from a man who saw life as serious and deeply absurd, and who drew on both to fuel his strong sense of purpose. "I've been a fan of Lincoln's from an early age," TV comic Conan O'Brien told TIME, "and really fascinated by him. The main thing for me is that he was really funny. He chose the right words and kept things short, and those are two secrets to being timelessly funny. My favorite example was after the battle of Chickamauga. One of the Union generals had behaved badly and had become unnerved. Lincoln said the general was 'confused and stunned like a duck hit on the head.' You don't have to think about that in the context of 1863. It's just a funny image—full of anger and bitterness but getting deeply to the truth too.

"If there was a fire in my house, I'd get my wife and child out, and then I'd run back in and get a Lincoln signature that I own—a pardon that he signed. I think I look at it every day." Asked why, he pauses for a second. "He's become such an otherworldly figure, such an iconic figure. But the fact is, he's a person. I guess it's inspiring to me that people are capable of being that cool." ∎

Life Behind the Lege 1d

Lincoln's journey from the frontier to Ford's Theatre

From his obscure birth to his shocking death, Abraham Lincoln provided all the ingredients for a myth that grows with each passing generation. A hardworking, self-taught farm boy grows up to become President, leads the nation through a wrenching cataclysm and is killed at the moment of victory.

Behind those bare facts are many Lincolns: lawyer, master politician, storyteller, warrior, jokester and man of near constant sorrow.

General William T. Sherman, no soft touch, provides one epitaph: "Of all the men I ever met, he seemed to possess more of the elements of greatness, combined with goodness, than any other."

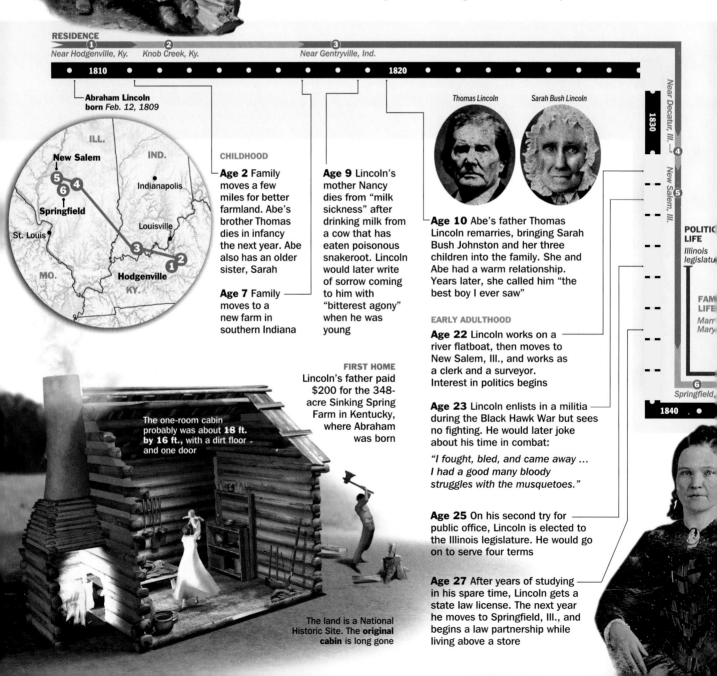

RESIDENCE

① Near Hodgenville, Ky.   ② Knob Creek, Ky.   ③ Near Gentryville, Ind.

1810   1820

Abraham Lincoln born Feb. 12, 1809

Thomas Lincoln   *Sarah Bush Lincoln*

Near Decatur, Ill. — 1830 ④

New Salem, Ill. ⑤

POLITIC LIFE
Illinois legislatu

FAM LIFE
Marr Mary

⑥ Springfield,

1840

CHILDHOOD

Age 2 Family moves a few miles for better farmland. Abe's brother Thomas dies in infancy the next year. Abe also has an older sister, Sarah

Age 7 Family moves to a new farm in southern Indiana

Age 9 Lincoln's mother Nancy dies from "milk sickness" after drinking milk from a cow that has eaten poisonous snakeroot. Lincoln would later write of sorrow coming to him with "bitterest agony" when he was young

Age 10 Abe's father Thomas Lincoln remarries, bringing Sarah Bush Johnston and her three children into the family. She and Abe had a warm relationship. Years later, she called him "the best boy I ever saw"

EARLY ADULTHOOD

Age 22 Lincoln works on a river flatboat, then moves to New Salem, Ill., and works as a clerk and a surveyor. Interest in politics begins

Age 23 Lincoln enlists in a militia during the Black Hawk War but sees no fighting. He would later joke about his time in combat:

"I fought, bled, and came away ... I had a good many bloody struggles with the musquetoes."

Age 25 On his second try for public office, Lincoln is elected to the Illinois legislature. He would go on to serve four terms

Age 27 After years of studying in his spare time, Lincoln gets a state law license. The next year he moves to Springfield, Ill., and begins a law partnership while living above a store

ILL.

New Salem

⑤ ④
⑥
Springfield

St. Louis

IND.

Indianapolis

Louisville

MO.   Hodgenville KY.

③
② ①

FIRST HOME
Lincoln's father paid $200 for the 348-acre Sinking Spring Farm in Kentucky, where Abraham was born

The one-room cabin probably was about **18 ft. by 16 ft.**, with a dirt floor and one door

The land is a National Historic Site. The **original cabin** is long gone

Lincoln on Lincoln

I was born Feb. 12, 1809, in Hardin County, Kentucky. My parents were both born in Virginia, of undistinguished families—second families, perhaps I should say. My mother, who died in my tenth year, was of a family of the name of Hanks, some of whom now reside in Adams, and others in Macon Counties, Illinois. My paternal grandfather, Abraham Lincoln, emigrated from Rockingham County, Virginia, to Kentucky, about 1781 or 2, where, a year or two later, he was killed by indians, not in battle, but by stealth, when he was laboring to open a farm in the forest.

My father, at the death of his father, was but six years of age; and he grew up, litterally without education. He removed from Kentucky to what is now Spencer County, Indiana, in my eighth year. We reached our new home about the time the State came into the Union. It was a wild region, with many bears and other wild animals, still in the woods. There I grew up. There were some schools, so called; but no qualification was ever required of a teacher beyond "readin', writin', and cipherin'" to the Rule of Three. If a straggler supposed to understand latin happened to sojourn in the neighborhood, he was looked upon as a wizzard. There was absolutely nothing to excite ambition for education. Of course when I came of age I did not know much. Still somehow, I could read, write, and cipher to the Rule of Three; but that was all. I have not been to school since. The little advance I now have upon this store of education, I have picked up from time to time under the pressure of necessity.

Abraham Lincoln wrote very little about his early life, but he did provide two brief autobiographies for use by newspapers when he ran for president in 1860. The passages above, published on Feb. 11, 1860, reveal Lincoln's ongoing regret at his lack of formal education (and pride in his self-education), 50 years after the fact. The spelling errors prove his point.

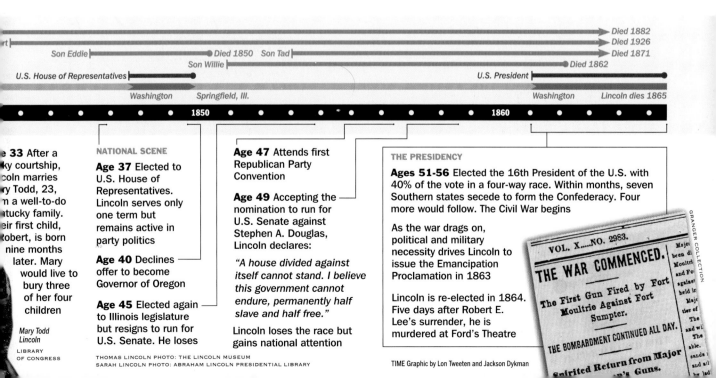

Died 1882
Died 1926
Son Eddie ● Died 1850 Son Tad Died 1871
Son Willie ● Died 1862
U.S. House of Representatives U.S. President

Washington Springfield, Ill. Washington Lincoln dies 1865

1850 1860

e 33 After a
ky courtship,
coln marries
ry Todd, 23,
m a well-to-do
tucky family.
eir first child,
Robert, is born
nine months
later. Mary
would live to
bury three
of her four
children

*Mary Todd
Lincoln*

NATIONAL SCENE

Age 37 Elected to
U.S. House of
Representatives.
Lincoln serves only
one term but
remains active in
party politics

Age 40 Declines
offer to become
Governor of Oregon

Age 45 Elected again
to Illinois legislature
but resigns to run for
U.S. Senate. He loses

Age 47 Attends first
Republican Party
Convention

Age 49 Accepting the
nomination to run for
U.S. Senate against
Stephen A. Douglas,
Lincoln declares:

*"A house divided against
itself cannot stand. I believe
this government cannot
endure, permanently half
slave and half free."*

Lincoln loses the race but
gains national attention

THE PRESIDENCY

Ages 51-56 Elected the 16th President of the U.S. with
40% of the vote in a four-way race. Within months, seven
Southern states secede to form the Confederacy. Four
more would follow. The Civil War begins

As the war drags on,
political and military
necessity drives Lincoln to
issue the Emancipation
Proclamation in 1863

Lincoln is re-elected in 1864.
Five days after Robert E.
Lee's surrender, he is
murdered at Ford's Theatre

VOL. X.....NO. 2983.

THE WAR COMMENCED.

The First Gun Fired by Fort
Moultrie Against Fort
Sumpter.

THE BOMBARDMENT CONTINUED ALL DAY.

Spirited Return from Major

Youth

Forged by the Frontier

Abraham Lincoln and America grew up together, and the character of both the man and the nation were shaped by the settling of the continent's western wilderness, the frontier. In Lincoln's youth, this verdant, developing zone was still well east of the Mississippi River, in the hills, forests and prairies of Kentucky, Tennessee, Indiana, Illinois, Ohio and Michigan, and it was still riven by conflicts between Native Americans and white settlers. Abraham's father Thomas Lincoln saw his own father killed by Indians in Kentucky. As a young man, Abraham Lincoln fought in the 1832 Black Hawk War against Sauk and Kickapoo Indians. As President, he sent U.S. troops to quell an 1862 Sioux uprising in Minnesota.

The young Lincoln was a frontiersman who split logs, built cabins, surveyed land and sold goods to settlers. He entered politics as a Whig, embracing the party's gospel of "internal improvements": the spending of government funds to improve transportation, agriculture and commerce on the frontier. Elected a U.S. Congressman from Illinois in 1846, he opposed President James K. Polk's land-grabbing war with Mexico on the frontier in the far Southwest, a stand so unpopular he gave up his seat. He stayed out of politics until a toxic question—whether slavery would be allowed in the frontier territories of Kansas and Nebraska—thrust him onto the national stage.

When he ran for the presidency, Lincoln became an icon: "the Rail Splitter," the log-cabin-born exemplar of homely frontier values. As President, he signed the Homestead Act of 1862, which awarded federal lands in the West to settlers ready to improve them. Lincoln's abiding vision of a Union always striving to make itself more perfect is the dream of a frontiersman, writ large.

Expansive vistas *This photograph of Tennessee's Lookout Mountain was taken in 1864, but the view would have been very similar in Lincoln's youth*

ABRAHAM LINCOLN BIRTHPLACE NATIONAL HISTORIC SITE

From Virginia Planters to Hard-Scrabble Settlers

Lincoln is a venerable name in England, where the capital of Lincolnshire in East Anglia is the home of a soaring Gothic cathedral. But Abraham Lincoln expressed little interest in tracing his family history back to England, for he viewed the Lincolns as less than venerable. His grandfather and namesake, Abraham, had sold a fine home in Virginia to follow America's westward impulse and settle in Kentucky, where he soon held claim to more than 5,000 acres of land. But in 1786, this first Abe Lincoln was killed by Indians while his youngest son, Thomas, 8, watched. Under the rules of primogeniture, the family's oldest son, Mordecai, inherited Abraham's entire state, and Thomas and older brother Josiah were left to fend for themselves.

The abrupt fall from grace forced Thomas Lincoln into a life of diligent toil as a carpenter, but he slowly scraped together enough money to buy a farm near Elizabethtown, Ky.—and to win the hand of Nancy Hanks, daughter of a local farming family. They married in 1806, when she was 22 and he was 28. Abraham Lincoln would come to believe that his mother was born out of wedlock, and most historians agree. Indeed, Lincoln found he had little in common with his father, whom he considered unambitious, and he liked to think he had inherited his inquisitive mind from his unknown grandfather on his mother's side.

Nancy Hanks gave birth to a daughter, Sarah, in 1807, and the small family later moved to a larger homestead, Sinking Spring Farm. It was here that Abraham Lincoln was born, on Feb. 12, 1809. When a dispute arose over the deed to the land, Thomas bought a smaller farm near Knob Creek, which had the added advantage of being more fertile. Abe Lincoln spent the next four years of his life here, amid the lush hills pictured above. The cabin shown above is a modern reconstruction, part of the Abraham Lincoln Birthplace, operated by the National Park Service.

Lincoln Logs

Thomas Lincoln's father Abraham sold the substantial Virginia homestead below to seek his fortune on the frontier. But his untimely death left Thomas impoverished, and Thomas' son, also Abraham, grew up in a succession of rude cabins on the Kentucky, Indiana and Illinois frontiers. His log-cabin nativity plays a major role in the mythology that has grown up around Lincoln; it is the necessary prelude to his inspirational rise as a self-made man. Lincoln's political image as the Rail Splitter was carefully crafted, but in glorifying his humble early life, his supporters were not breaking the mold but following it. In the years after Andrew Jackson became the first President to have made his name on the frontier, many candidates sought the mantle of virtue associated with such uncitified, and thus pure, origins.

There is no doubt that Lincoln's origins were indeed humble. He told an inquiring newspaperman that the story of his early life could be summed up by a line from Thomas Gray's famous *Elegy:* "The short and simple annals of the poor." Indeed, when the Lincoln family moved from Kentucky to Indiana when Abe was 7, they spent the first days near Little Pigeon Creek in a large lean-to that was enclosed by logs on three sides but open to the winds on the fourth.

None of the various cabins Lincoln lived in are still standing. The illustration above is said to show the cabin in which Thomas Lincoln first settled his family in Illinois in 1830. The cabin below was built by Thomas and Abe Lincoln when the senior Lincolns made their final move to Coles County, Ill., in 1831. Here Thomas died in 1851. His son Abe did not attend his funeral.

CONTEMPORARY VOICES

"On the subject of his ancestry and origin I only remember one time when Mr. Lincoln ever referred to it … He said, among other things, that [his mother] was the illegitimate daughter of Lucy Hanks and a well-bred Virginia farmer or planter; and he argued that from this last source came his power of analysis, his logic, his mental activity, his ambition, and all the qualities that distinguished him from the other members and descendants of the Hanks family." —WILLIAM HERNDON

Foundering Father

The life of Thomas Lincoln, Abraham's father, is a study in mobility, too little of it upward. The senior Lincoln's flat-lining trajectory complicated his relationship with his son, who was consumed with dreams of self-improvement. Indeed, Abraham's youth is the chronicle of his father's ongoing search for greener pastures. In 1811, when Abe was 2, the family moved from his Kentucky birthplace, the Sinking Spring Farm, where the soil was poor, to a better patch of land ten miles away on Knob Creek. The farming here was better, but in five years Thomas Lincoln uprooted his family again, and they crossed the Ohio River and settled in Little Pigeon Creek in southern Indiana in 1816. This move, Abraham later came to believe, was spurred by Thomas' problems in proving his land ownership in Kentucky as well as his opposition to slavery. That hatred of human bondage, perhaps based in Thomas' Baptist faith, may have been his most lasting contribution to his son's personality.

Not long after the family moved to Indiana, Nancy Hanks Lincoln died after consuming poisoned milk. Left to care for Abe, 9 and Sarah, 11, Thomas wooed and married the widow Sarah Bush Johnston, a sensible mother of three who merged her family with Thomas' and became a profound influence on Abraham. The marriage was a step up for Thomas, but after a few years of renewed vigor, he drifted into a life of lassitude and ill health. Relations between father and son became strained during Abe's teenage years, when by law any money he earned had to be given to Thomas, who often hired him out as a laborer. Perhaps worse in Abe's view, Thomas did little to encourage his son's love of learning. In Thomas' defense, Abe simply didn't fit the mold of pioneer boy: he not only spent all his free time reading, he refused to hunt game after he shot and killed a wild turkey at age 7.

In 1830 Thomas decided once again to pull up stakes and head west. A year later, Abe helped Thomas and Sarah build the cabin in Coles County, Ill., 10 miles south of Charleston, that would be Thomas' last home. Now 21, Abe struck out to make his own way in life. Though he provided monetary support to Thomas in the decades that followed, Abraham Lincoln, by then a prosperous lawyer, did not make the journey of several days it would have required to attend his father's funeral in 1851. Lincoln biographer David Herbert Donald sums up the father-son relationship by noting, "In all of his published writings, and indeed, even in reports of hundreds of stories and conversations, [Abraham] had not one favorable word to say about his father."

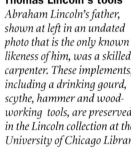

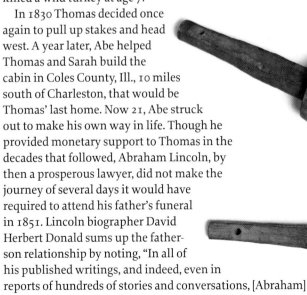

Thomas Lincoln's tools
Abraham Lincoln's father, shown at left in an undated photo that is the only known likeness of him, was a skilled carpenter. These implements, including a drinking gourd, scythe, hammer and wood-working tools, are preserved in the Lincoln collection at the University of Chicago Library

R.I.P. *Nancy Hanks Lincoln's first grave site bore only a rude marker; this tombstone dates from early in the 20th century. The grave is located at the Lincoln Boyhood National Memorial outside Gentryville, Ind. At right is the only known image of Sarah Bush Johnston Lincoln; it is undated*

A Tale of Two Mothers

Nancy Hanks Lincoln died at age 34 of a disease the people of the frontier called "the milk-sick" on Oct. 5, 1818, when her son Abraham was only 9. Her Kentucky cousins Thomas and Elizabeth Sparrow, who had recently joined the Lincoln family at Little Pigeon Creek in Indiana, bringing more hands and valued companionship to the small settlement, preceded her in death from the same cause by only a few days. The settlers didn't understand the intestinal ailment that killed swiftly but believed it had to do with the milk they drank. They were correct: much later it was discovered that the disease was passed along when cattle ate poisonous snakeroot plants.

There is no portrait from life of Thomas Lincoln's first wife, and photography was several decades in the future. And since Abraham Lincoln committed very few of his early memories to paper, Nancy Hanks Lincoln remains an elusive figure.

We know far more about the woman who became a prominent, positive influence on young Abe, his stepmother Sarah Bush Johnston Lincoln. She entered Abe's life abruptly, for it is a truth universally acknowledged that a widower in possession of two young children to raise on the frontier must be in want of a wife, and Thomas Lincoln was no exception.

Within a year of Nancy Lincoln's death, he returned to Elizabethtown, Ky., in search of a bride. There he renewed the acquaintance of an old friend, Sarah Bush Johnston, 30, whose husband Daniel Johnston had died in 1816, leaving her with three children to raise. Their courtship may not have been as swift as the one described in the traditional Southern tune *Down the Old Plank Road*—"My wife died on Friday night/ Saturday she was buried/ Sunday was my courtin' day/ Monday I was married"—but it was brief and businesslike. Thomas Lincoln settled the debts Sarah had been unable to pay after Daniel's death, packed his new bride, her children and her belongings into an ox-cart and set out for Indiana.

When Sarah and her young children Elizabeth, John D., and Matilda arrived in the rude clearing in the Indiana woods, they brought possessions that must have seemed wondrous to Abe and sister Sarah: forks and spoons, a walnut bureau and a spinning wheel. Their new stepmother quickly set to work improving the homestead—and the children. Both younger than 12, Abe and Sarah had spent several months living with their cousin Dennis Hanks alone in the wilds of Indiana. Now they were bathed and given new clothes; the one-room cabin was given a new floor, a new loft for the children to sleep in and, like the kids, a thorough cleaning.

But Sarah's cleansing, uplifting influence made its most significant impact on her stepson, for she, like Abe, believed in the power of learning. Unlike Thomas Lincoln, and despite her own illiteracy, she encouraged Abe's growing fondness for reading and the life of the mind. Sarah and Abe were soulmates who grew to be very close, even as Abe and his father drifted further apart. In years to come, Abe would visit Sarah when his travels as a circuit-riding lawyer took him near the home where she and Thomas settled in Coles County, Ill. After he was elected President, Lincoln made time before leaving for Washington to visit his stepmother. Sarah was now 72, once again a widow and living with her daughter in Farmington, Ill. The emotional reunion was their last meeting.

In September 1865 another visitor came to her cabin. Lincoln's law partner and biographer William Herndon visited the aged woman and sat for hours, harvesting for posterity her irreplaceable memories of Abe's youth. She died four years later.

"Abe never gave me a cross word or look and never refused in fact, or even in appearance, to do anything I requested him. I never gave him a cross word in all my life ... his mind and mine ... seemed to move together." —SARAH BUSH JOHNSTON LINCOLN

Lincoln's copy-book *Sarah Bush Lincoln gave William Herndon these pages from young Abe's copy-book after the President was assassinated*

The Allure of Learning

The fanciful portrait at left, painted by Eastman Johnson in 1868 as veneration of the late President was on the rise, accurately depicts the youthful Abe as a boy enraptured by books, even if it does suit him up in duds fit for a fancy Eastern scholar rather than an Indiana settler. Lincoln's love of learning, his determination to improve his mind, was one of the defining characteristics of his youth, along with the outgoing personality that made him a natural storyteller, cracker of jokes and writer of poetic parodies—and the growth spurt early in his teen years that turned him into a towering, gangly figure who left a memorable impression on everyone who met him.

Much of what we know about Lincoln as a young student comes from William Herndon's biography, and if the details sound burnished for posterity, they are not: Lincoln's love of reading and his intellectual rigor remained driving influences throughout his life. "His chief delight during the day," Herndon wrote after interviewing Sarah Bush Lincoln and other intimates of the young Abe, "was to lie down under the shade of some inviting tree to read and study. At night, lying on his stomach in front of the open fireplace, with a piece of charcoal he would cipher on a broad wooden shovel…his stepmother told me he devoured everything in the book line within his reach. If in his reading he came across anything that pleased his fancy, he entered it down in a

copy-book—a sort of repository, in which he was wont to store everything worthy of preservation."

John Hanks, a relative of Nancy Hanks Lincoln who settled in Indiana near the Lincoln family, was one of Abe's closest friends in his youth. He told Herndon, "When Abe and I returned to the house from work he would go to the cupboard, snatch a piece of corn bread, sit down, take a book, cock his legs up as high as his head and read…Whenever Abe had a chance in the field while at work, or at the house, he would stop and read. He kept the Bible and *Aesop's Fables* always within reach, and read them over and over again."

Abraham Lincoln was not merely a self-made man; he was a self-taught man. His formal schooling amounted to three brief spells in local schools, for his time had to be devoted to the grinding labors that helped his family survive. Looking back as an adult, the autodidact described these institutions as "schools, so-called…[where] no qualification was required of a teacher." Among the other books Lincoln is known to have read in his adolescence were John Bunyan's popular *Pilgrim's Progress*, Parson Weems' biography of George Washington, Benjamin Franklin's autobiography and a book of lessons in elocution, in whose pages he may first have made the acquaintance of his favorite author, William Shakespeare.

Have Ax, Will Chop

The image of Lincoln in his iconic role as "the Rail Splitter" has changed very little since it was first employed to present him as an uncorrupted product of the frontier when he was nominated to run for President in 1860. Here are three versions.

At near right is a life-size painting by an unknown artist, dating from Lincoln's political campaigns; this early version emphasizes the young man's toil.

At far right is an oil painting by J.L.G. Ferris from 1909, the centennial of Lincoln's birth; an open book awaits a rest period. At left is a 1965 painting by the noted illustrator Norman Rockwell, which puts the book into Lincoln's hand.

Tall Tales

Lincoln's teen years were spent in constant toil, as he juggled the physical labors demanded of all frontier people with the mental exertions he imposed on himself. He was only 11, contemporaries report, when he first began to shoot up in size, topping out at 6 ft. 4 in. at age 17. All his life, Lincoln had a towering physical presence that made him a memorable, unique character; the photo on the title page of this book, in which he looms over General John A. McClernand and security officer Allan Pinkerton at Antietam, reveals the extent to which his height made him a commanding figure.

Lincoln's devotion to reading and study set him apart among other youngsters on the frontier, but his size and physical strength ensured that no one mistook him for a dandy. In his teens, he began to circulate around the frontier settlements near Gentryville, Ind., visiting grain mills, taking in horse races and log-rollings. Once, when a stepbrother was losing a fight, he uncharacteristically

stepped into the circle, heaved the adversary out of it, swung a liquor bottle over his head and declared himself "the big buck of the lick," ready to take on all comers. Stories that were perhaps exaggerated and polished in retrospect have him performing prodigious feats of strength: holding an ax at arm's length for long minutes, carrying logs that three other men couldn't lift, hefting an entire hogshead of liquor. An amalgam of raw strength and a sharp mind, he fascinated those he met.

By his late teens, this backwoods Bunyan was becoming known for other qualities as well: wherever the frontier folk gathered, he was a galvanizing storyteller and conversationalist who wrote elaborate poems and parodies for social affairs and was once scolded by his father for amusing his pals by imitating a hell-raising Baptist preacher. Meanwhile, alone in the woods, his self-education continued: taking an interest in politics, he began practicing oratory on a tree-stump rostrum.

Finding His Bearings

By his late teen years, Abraham Lincoln had become restless; he chafed at the legal restrictions that bound him to his father's service until he was 21, and he increasingly sought broader horizons. His escape route, it turned out, was the rivers and streams of Indiana and Illinois. When he was 17, he and a friend set themselves up as sawyers, purveying firewood to steamboats plying the Ohio River; when that plan failed, he took a job ferrying passengers to passing boats and built a rude flatboat to do so. After two men tossed him dollar coins for a lift, he recalled years later, "The world seemed wider and fairer before me."

Thomas Lincoln also had new vistas on his mind, and early in 1830, just as Abe was turning 21, he helped Thomas and his stepmother Sarah move from Indiana to Macon County in central Illinois; their new homestead was 10 miles north of Decatur on the Sangamon River.

Abe struck out on his own as a riverman, and it was this new career that brought him to the village he would call home in his early 20s: New Salem, Ill. His arrival made quite an impression; he and two friends grounded a flatboat on which they were hauling freight on a dam across the Sangamon River at the New Salem mill. That's Lincoln at the left of the 20th century illustration at right; the former railsplitter has traded his ax for an an auger. Abe proceeded to bore a hole in the boat, allowing water that had flowed into it to drain out and lifting the vessel from the dam. The locals who had come out to watch the free entertainment were much impressed with this show of ingenuity.

That summer, Lincoln gave his first public speech outside a general store in Decatur, on a subject understandably close to his heart: he advocated the dredging and clearing of the Sangamon to allow more commerce to flow over it. This position revealed him to be aligned with the Whig Party, which argued for just such government initiatives.

Downstream *The picture above shows a Mississippi River flatboat from the 1890s; it is larger and more complex than the two vessels Lincoln would have taken down the river in 1828 and 1831, but it offers a sense of crew life on such boats. At far left is an advertisement for a slave sale at a New Orleans auction house; at near left is a Currier & Ives lithograph of the Crescent City some 20 years after Lincoln's visits. Throughout the 19th century, New Orleans was one of the world's busiest and most cosmopolitan port cities*

Down the Mississippi

When Abe Lincoln's flatboat ran aground on a mill dam in New Salem, Ill., the young man was starting out on the second of two journeys that first exposed him to an entirely different America: in 1828 and again in 1831, he traveled by flatboat down the Mississippi River to New Orleans. These visits gave the intellectually curious backwoodsman his first taste of urban life, for New Orleans was one of America's busiest ports and largest cities, with a population of 40,000. They also brought Lincoln for the first time into close contact with slavery, the "peculiar institution" of the South that would become the political and moral fulcrum of his life and presidency.

Lincoln's first trip down America's great river took place in 1828, when he was 19 years old and beginning to spread his wings. With his father's approval, he signed on as the only "bow hand" on a flatboat owned by the founder of Gentryville, Ill., James Gentry, and operated by his son Allen. The cargo was grain and meat; Lincoln's pay was $8 a month and board. Biographer and longtime confidant William Herndon claims Lincoln seldom spoke of this journey; the only event he recounted to Herndon involved a group of marauding blacks, apparently escapees from slavery, who attacked the boat while it was tied up at a plantation dock below Baton Rouge. Lincoln and Gentry picked up clubs, drove off the attackers, pursued them briefly, then returned to the boat and floated away from danger.

Three years later, now 22 and freed from his obligations to his father, Lincoln again made the journey by flatboat to New Orleans, this time on a larger craft that Abe, his late mother's relative John Hanks and his stepbrother James Johnston built at the behest of Denton Offutt. This larger-than-life character, part entrepreneur and part blowhard, operated various enterprises throughout central Illinois and would play an important role in Lincoln's early life. After their misadventure at New Salem, the boatmen had an uneventful trip to New Orleans, where they spent a month before returning to Illinois. One can only imagine the impact these two visits must have made upon the young frontiersmen. New Orleans, then as now, was a unique American city, a multiracial, colorful bazaar where ships of all nations docked, the French influence remained strong, and a colorful cast of characters sashayed through the streets: Creoles and Cajuns, Caribbean islanders and British tars, plantation owners, gamblers—and gangs of chained slaves bound for the auction block.

This longer sojourn in the Crescent City gave Lincoln his first extended view of slavery in practice, and he did not like what he saw. Herndon tells the story of Lincoln's viewing a young black woman being inspected like an animal at a slave auction and saying to Hanks, "By god, boys, let's get away from this. If ever I get a chance to hit that thing [meaning slavery], I'll hit it hard." Some historians claim this story is far too tidy (Hanks appears to have left New Orleans shortly after his arrival) and suspect that Herndon, who was more of an abolitionist than Lincoln, may have burnished or invented it. Yet there is no doubt that Lincoln hated the practice of slavery on moral grounds, and these first encounters with it surely left their mark. But Lincoln's two early trips down the Mississippi remain relatively unilluminated.

Little Town in the Big Woods

When Abraham Lincoln first encountered the hard-drinking, ever scheming entrepreneur Denton Offutt, who was 6 years his senior, he ran smack into his future. It was Offutt who commissioned Lincoln's second journey to New Orleans, in 1831, and he joined the group, growing to admire the younger man's enterprise. Upon their return, he proposed to set up Lincoln as a storekeeper in New Salem, and Abe agreed. Years later, comparing himself to the vessel that ran aground on the dam at New Salem, Lincoln remarked to William Herndon that at the time he had been "a piece of floating driftwood; that after the winter of deep snow, he had come down the river with the freshet … and, aimlessly floating about, he had accidentally lodged at New Salem."

New Salem was just putting down roots itself. Founded only the year before, in 1830, it occupied the high ground atop a tall bluff over the Sangamon River, and its roughly 100 inhabitants sold goods and produce and offered essential services to settlers for miles around. A typical frontier town, it boasted mills, a post office, a few stores, a blacksmith, a school, a cooper and, of course, a tavern or two. Abe Lincoln would spend the next six years here, having the formative experiences of his 20s: the gangling jack-of-all-trades was at various times a militia officer, a postmaster, an election clerk, a storekeeper, a surveyor, a candidate for the state legislature. In lean times, he returned to splitting rails. And here he first fell in love.

Ironically, the river that brought Lincoln to New Salem and promised to be its commercial link to the wider world wasn't up to the job: though Lincoln won acclaim when he helped pilot a steamboat to the village's landing in 1832, the Sangamon was too shallow to support large vessels, and the efforts of Lincoln and others to have the government dredge it failed. Bypassed by the railroads and unsuited for river trade, New Salem went into decline not long after Lincoln moved away: its glory days were over.

Bygone days *Well before Lincoln's death, the village of New Salem was deserted and in ruins. Like Williamsburg in Virginia, it has been reconstructed as a historical tourist attraction that, although artificial, can evoke a strong sense of how life was lived here in the 1830s*

Records *Above right, Berry and Lincoln's tavern license. At left is the promissory note signed by the two merchants for what Lincoln jokingly called "the national debt." At top is a picture of an early reconstruction of the Lincoln-Berry store; at top right is a restored version of the back room of the store, the living quarters for the two men*

Abraham Lincoln, Proprietor

When Captain Lincoln returned to New Salem from the Black Hawk War, he was out of a job: Denton Offutt's general store had failed just before Lincoln enlisted. But Abe and a fellow veteran of the war, William F. Berry, soon arranged to buy an interest in one of the three other stores then operating in the town, and during the winter they further acquired the goods and building of the town's second-best store, co-signing a promissory note for $650, a hefty price in 1833—with nothing down. Business was slow, so they applied for a liquor license, though Lincoln's signature on the application may not be in his hand, suggesting the profligate Berry may have forged it. In later years, Lincoln the politician would be haunted by the charge that he had been a tavern keeper, costing him the votes of teetotalers. Much later, when prohibitionists claimed Lincoln as one of their own, barkeeps across America hung up framed copies of his liquor license.

But the store failed, just as New Salem itself began to fail, owing to its poor location. Lincoln struggled through the rest of a bleak winter until he managed to win an appointment as New Salem's postmaster. The job paid little, but Lincoln felt enriched: increasingly fascinated by politics, he now had access to every newspaper mailed to town. He soon landed a new position as a county surveyor, a good match for his rigorous cast of mind, and he excelled at the work. But as the note he and Berry had signed to open their store came due, a judge ordered Lincoln's personal possessions attached, including his surveying tools (a kind-hearted older friend later bought them at auction and returned them). Matters got worse when Berry died without warning; though legally bound for only half the debt, Lincoln promised he would pay it all. His interest in politics had long been an avocation; now he realized that it might—it must!—become a profitable vocation.

"While Lincoln at one end of the store was dispensing political information, Berry at the other was disposing of the firm's liquors, being the best customer for that article of merchandise himself."

—WILLIAM HERNDON

Of Arms and the Man

America's future Commander-in-Chief had his closest brush with conflict in the Black Hawk War of 1832, when some 500 braves of the Sauk tribe, led by the charismatic chief Black Hawk, left their reservation in today's Iowa and crossed the Mississippi into Illinois in May 1832, sparking panic among white settlers and leading Illinois governor John Reynolds to call up the militia. When enlistees from New Salem were organized into the Fourth Regiment of Mounted Volunteers of the State of Illinois, they elected Abe Lincoln their captain, an honor that moved him so much that he later recalled, "Not since had any success in life afforded me so much satisfaction."

In later years, Lincoln never failed to make light of his soldiering days, claiming his most ferocious foes were insects. Of his career as an officer, he told William Herndon: "To the first order given to one of [his charges], he received the response, 'Go to the devil, Sir!'" By August the war was over: Black Hawk and his band were chased into Wisconsin, where many of them were massacred. Lincoln was paid a lump sum of $125 for his service, and he also received a grant of 40 acres in Iowa in 1852 and another for 120 acres in Illinois in 1856. His son Robert sold them both for $13,000 in 1892.

Lincoln returned to New Salem with his personal fortunes little changed: he lost the race for the legislative seat he had begun before enlisting, and though he may have enjoyed the hero's send-off depicted in the 20th century illustration above, his return was inglorious: Lincoln's horse was stolen as the soldiers broke camp, and he walked and canoed the 250 miles home.

Mack-a-tai-mish-e-kiah-kiak,
or Black Hawk,
A Sauk Chief

WHAT LINCOLN SAID

"If [a fellow soldier] saw any live fighting Indians, it was more than I did; but I had a good many bloody struggles with the mosquitoes. I am a military hero ... I fought, bled, and came away."

A failed uprising *The map above traces key engagements of the summer-long war—none of which involved Lincoln and his New Salem regiment. At left is Black Hawk, a notable chief who first fought Americans as an ally of the British in the War of 1812. He was captured in the final conflict of the 1832 war, the Battle of Bad Axe, named for the river where it took place, and he and a number of other captives were then paraded before large, jeering crowds in Washington and other Eastern cities. As President, Lincoln would deal with an even more consequential Indian uprising in 1862, against Sioux and Kickapoo tribes in Minnesota.*

Lincoln's First Love

It's hard to keep secrets in a town as small as New Salem, so at some point in 1835, most of the villagers were aware that one of the town's most popular residents, Abe Lincoln, had fallen in love with Ann Mayes Rutledge, daughter of James Rutledge, one of New Salem's co-founders and owner of a thriving, two-story tavern and hostelry. Ann, we're told, was a short, attractive, lively woman whom Lincoln first met when she was in her teens. When they fell in love and perhaps planned to marry, she was 22 and Abe was 26. Ann had previously had an "understanding" with another young man, John McNamar, who called himself McNeil in New Salem and was less than truthful in other ways. Neighbors said it was after he left the village that Abe—whose awkwardness in the face of eligible women was part of his charm—began to court Ann.

But this happy tale of young love has a sad ending. In the summer of 1835, Ann came down with a fever, now believed to be typhoid. After a brief illness, she died on Aug. 25. Lincoln, who had lost his mother when he was only 9, and whose sister Sarah died in childbirth in 1828, now faced the loss of his first love. He was more than distraught; he could not bear to think of rain falling on Ann's grave, he told friends. He wandered in the woods with a gun, so depressed that neighbors began to fear he might take his life. Local farmer Henry McHenry told Lincoln's biographer William Herndon, "As to the condition of Lincoln's Mind after the death of Miss R., … this gloom seemed to deepen for some time, so as to give anxiety to his friends in regard to his Mind." Indeed, those friends urged him to visit an older, married couple in the area, Bowling Green and wife Nancy, who took Lincoln in and nursed him back to health over a period of weeks. This was the first of two major mental breakdowns Lincoln would experience; he was subject to periods of acute psychological depression throughout his life.

Young love—or not? *Above, a modern artist working in a faux-primitive style imagines Lincoln and Rutledge as a courting couple. At top right is a signed grammar book Lincoln gave her; it is the only artifact of their acquaintance.*

But is the story as faux as the painting? Over the years, some respected historians have called tales of the romance overheated: it remains a divisive issue among Lincoln scholars. It was first told a few years after Lincoln's death by his law partner William Herndon, based on his interviews with Lincoln's oldest acquaintances. Mary Todd Lincoln (who disliked Herndon) and son Robert called it bogus. Today most scholars believe Herndon's account is correct in its essentials. Joshua Wolf Shenk thoroughly explores the issues surrounding the tale in his 2005 book, Lincoln's Melancholy.

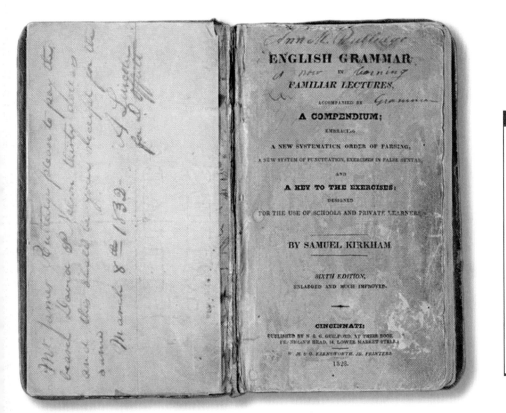

CONTEMPORARY VOICES

"The effect upon Mr. Lincoln's mind was terrible. He became plunged in despair, and many of his friends feared that reason would desert her throne."

—ROBERT RUTLEDGE,
BROTHER OF ANN RUTLEDGE

A Farcical Romance

Following the death of Ann Rutledge, Lincoln conducted an on-again, off-again romance with a well-born, well-educated Kentucky woman, Mary Owens. He had met this dark-eyed, quick-witted brunette when she visited New Salem to see a sister in 1833 or '34, before Lincoln's doomed love affair with Ann Rutledge played itself out. When she returned to New Salem in 1836, perhaps lured by accounts that Lincoln admired her, the two began a courtship, apparently conducted with a characteristic mixture of both zeal and reluctance on Abe's part.

After Lincoln moved to Springfield, Ill., in 1837, he sent her the letter at right, in which he finally broke off the relationship, writing, "For the purpose of making the matter as plain as possible, I now say, that you can now drop the subject, dismiss your thoughts (if you ever had any) from me forever, and leave this letter unanswered." She did.

Up to speed *Above is a Currier & Ives lithograph of a steamboat "wooding up" with fuel on the Mississippi in 1863, 50 years after the powerful ships first began traveling America's rivers. At left is a Baltimore & Ohio locomotive in 1848; railroads began to reshape U.S. society in the 1830s.*

As a Whig, Lincoln enthusiastically supported the transportation revolution. In 1832 he helped pilot a steamboat up the Sangamon River to New Salem in Illinois, thrilling residents of the isolated village. But the Sangamon lacked the natural flow to support year-round shipping, and the town failed. In his lawyering years, railroads would be among Lincoln's most important clients, and as President he signed the law that chartered the first railroad to span the continent.

The Acceleration of America

Abe Lincoln was born into Daniel Boone's America, where distance was measured by how far a man with an oxcart could travel in a day. Lincoln's early journeys through Indiana and Illinois were made on foot or by canoe, raft or flatboat. But even as Lincoln was reaching manhood, new technologies were radically transforming the U.S., growing its wealth, abolishing old concepts of distance and accelerating the pace of daily life. The foremost driver of change was the steam engine, a potent generator of energy that was mounted first on vessels and later on rails.

As steamboat and railroad technologies advanced, they boosted commerce, created vast new fortunes, showered prosperity on the routes they traveled, opened the frontier to a surge of new development and helped unite the states as never before, knitting them together in a newly complex economic network. Cotton from the South could now travel to New England's textile mills; natural resources were shipped from west to east to be turned into finished goods, which were then shipped west again. The Illinois of Lincoln's youth was a wilderness slowly being settled, but by the 1840s Chicago was becoming a booming colossus of trade that spread its nourishing tentacles of railroad and steamboat lines throughout the nation, down the Mississippi and across the Great Lakes.

The Reign of King Cotton

Blessed with an abundance and variety of natural resources and enthralled by new technologies, the increasingly urban Northern states of the Union created ever more diverse economies in the 1830s and '40s. But in the states of the deep South, a single crop, cotton, dominated the economy and shaped society. The worldwide demand for cotton made fortunes for the owners of vast Southern plantations. Yet the reliance on cotton exports became a straitjacket that bound the planters ever more tightly to slavery, the system of cheap labor upon which plantation economies were built. The cotton-exporting states of the U.S. South played as important a role in the global economy of the first half of the 19th century as did the petroleum-exporting countries of the Middle East in the second half of the 20th century. "Much of Atlantic civilization in the 19th century was built on the back of the enslaved field hand," historian Daniel Walker Howe noted in his 2007 study of American life from 1815-48, *What Hath God Wrought.*

Southern planters took great pride in their agrarian economy and the culture it made possible; so much so that they preferred to continue exporting raw cotton out of their region to be turned into finished goods by others, rather than introduce factory systems to create cotton textiles at home. The South's fate hinged on this choice, for the stark economic differences between the technologically advanced North and the agrarian South would prove a critical factor in the North's eventual victory in the Civil War.

Fiber of life *Cotton from the South was shipped across the ocean to Britain and north to New England, where textile mills like the one in Massachusetts shown in the circa 1836 illustration below were among the first factories of the Industrial Revolution. The states of the South exported so much cotton to England that Confederates expected the English would rally to their side during the Civil War out of economic necessity*

A Clash of Cultures in the Southwest

Even as Abe Lincoln was coming of age in Illinois, the young U.S. was experiencing growing pains of its own. Ironically, it was America's great natural gift—the enormous stretch of land to the West, beckoning a growing nation across the continent—that became the focus of debate over its most unnatural practice, the institution of slavery that increasingly divided the states of North and South. By tacit agreement, the issue of slavery was addressed only obliquely in the Constitution; slaves were regarded as part of the "property" protected in it, and they were referred to as "other persons." By 1820, when Lincoln was only 11, the growing divisions over slavery—hated by many in the North—almost led to a schism between the states. The Missouri Compromise patched up the wounds temporarily: Missouri was admitted to the Union as a slave state and Maine as a free state, while slavery was forbidden in the other territories acquired by the Louisiana Purchase lying north of the southern border of Missouri.

But political upheaval in an area that was not part of the Purchase revealed the fragility of the attempts to keep slave and nonslave states roughly equal in political influence. Through the 1820s and '30s, slaveholding Americans began settling in today's Texas, then a province of Mexico, where human slavery had been outlawed in 1829. As their numbers increased, "Texians" revolted against Mexican rule, declaring their independence in 1836. Superior Mexican power overwhelmed the Texian stronghold called the Alamo on March 6, 1836 (above)—but the Texians later drove the Mexican army from the new Republic of Texas. This republic sought to be annexed into the U.S. as a slave state but was not admitted until 1845. Texas joined the Confederacy in the Civil War.

Old Hickory's America

Andrew Jackson bestrode the growing U.S. like a colossus in the first half of the 19th century. Born in 1767, he soared to fame after he beat a British force in the 1814 Battle of New Orleans, fought shortly after the War of 1812 officially ended. A slave-owning Tennessean, Jackson was a ruthless Indian fighter and a strong believer in America's territorial expansion.

As the political party system in the U.S. developed, Jackson became the leader of the Democrats, who supported slavery and its extension. Though he won the popular vote when he ran for President in 1824, the election was stalemated in the Electoral College, and the House of

Representatives voted to make John Quincy Adams President; Jackson's allies called it a "corrupt bargain."

But Jackson won election in 1828, and in his two terms he left a strong stamp on the nation. The first frontier President often supported state's rights, but when South Carolina claimed it could "nullify" federal laws, Jackson stood firm until the state legislature backed down. Americans came in two stripes in the 1820s-40s: you either hated or loved Jackson. Lincoln, a Whig, was no lover of "Old Hickory."

The Evolving Party System

Abraham Lincoln's great political hero was Henry Clay, the Kentucky Senator who devoted his career to preserving the Union. As a Kentuckian, Clay represented a border state where slavery was legal but whose topography wasn't suited

to the plantation economies of the deep South and thus never became a captive of King Cotton. As a young Senator, Clay helped craft the Missouri Compromise, which kept the Union together and settled, for more than three decades, the question of slavery's extension to the frontier territories.

As America's party system evolved during the 1830s and '40s, Clay emerged as a leader of the Whig Party and the nation's most prominent opponent of Andrew Jackson's Democratic Party. Whigs opposed the spread of slavery, and they pursued a vision of the U.S. as laid out in Polk's "American System": a growing, prosperous nation focused on commerce and cities rather than farms and agriculture, with a strong congressional branch (as opposed to Jackson's powerful Executive model). Whigs championed government investment in internal improvements: the roads, canals, turnpikes and railroads that would stitch the nation together in a vast network of commerce.

In the 1836 election, Whig candidate William Henry Harrison, the Indian-fighting war hero, wasn't strong enough to defeat Jackson's handpicked successor, Martin Van Buren. In 1840 the party passed over Clay and chose Harrison again, and this time he defeated Van Buren, who had presided over the catastrophic economic panic of 1837. But Harrison died only a month after taking office, and his successor, John Tyler, effectively abandoned the Whig program. Lincoln had supported Clay for the Whig candidacy in 1840 but, as a good party man, he lent strong support to Harrison when he became the nominee. Lincoln traveled throughout Illinois making speeches for Harrison, and for a powerful national bank—an idea that was anathema to Jacksonian Democrats.

As for Clay, he finally ran for the presidency in 1844 but lost to James K. Polk, the strong Jackson Democrat known as "Young Hickory." But Clay would take an active role in once again brokering harmony among the bickering states as one of the proponents of the Compromise of 1850.

Making a Name for Himself in Vandalia

The residents of New Salem were impressed with the ambition and drive of their new neighbor, Abe Lincoln, and in 1832, when Lincoln was only 23, friends who had heard him speak his mind on politics urged him to run for the Illinois state legislature. Lincoln agreed, but when he rode off to serve in the Black Hawk War, his candidacy sputtered out. Two years later, Lincoln, in need of the income a seat in the legislature would bring, mounted a serious campaign for office, running as a Whig. His campaigning amounted to traveling the countryside, shaking hands and chatting with voters. When he asked farmhands harvesting grain for their support, they retorted that they had no use for soft-handed politicians. Lincoln grabbed a scythe, made a circuit of the field, and won their votes. Both Lincoln and an admirer who was fast becoming a mentor, John Todd Stuart, were elected.

   Lincoln bought himself his first suit of clothes for his new position; the formal duds must have been a gratifying reminder of how far he had risen from the dirt-floor cabins of his youth. Once in the capital, the smallish town of Vandalia (pop. 850), he stayed in the background, a diligent backbencher sizing up his new world. When the session adjourned, he resumed his surveying career in New Salem. His constituents liked Lincoln, and he was handily re-elected in 1836. During the campaign, he delivered a rousing speech at a Springfield rally that showed his rising command of oratory. In his second term he became the floor leader of the Whig faction in the House, as well as the leader of the "Long Nine," the seven representatives and two senators who composed the Sangamon County delegation and were so named because they were each above average in height. Showing a real flair for political dealing, Lincoln helped pass two successful initiatives in the 1837 session. The "Long Nine" succeeded in their parochial push to move the state capital to Springfield. And the legislature approved a very ambitious plan of internal improvements under which the state borrowed $10 million to build a vast network of railroads, canals and bridges. But the plan was quickly derailed by a nationwide financial panic, the projects were never built, the state was left deeply in debt—and Lincoln and his fellow Whigs, so recently elated by the passage of their long-sought agenda, were utterly discredited.

Hat in the ring *The ticket at right showing Whig candidates for the 1834 Illinois legislature is one of the earliest known artifacts of Lincoln's political career. Just above his name is that of John Todd Stuart, an older, respected Springfield attorney whom Lincoln had met in the Black Hawk War, where Stuart served as one of Lincoln's superior officers. Stuart was among those who urged Lincoln to run, and he also suggested that Lincoln begin the study of law. Three years later, Lincoln joined Stuart's firm in Springfield as an apprentice lawyer. The two Whigs were leaders of the "Long Nine" legislators who pushed through the 1837 program of public works that ended up putting the state deeply in debt.*

At left is a statehouse that was never used; the citizens of small, out-of-the-way Vandalia built it in 1836-37 in their effort to retain the city's status as the capital city of Illinois, but when the Sangamon County faction succeeded in moving the capital to Springfield, thanks in large part to Lincoln's mastery of political give-and-take, it also awarded $15,000 to the town of Vandalia to recoup its investment.

The model *Illinois Whigs seeking to demonstrate how investment in internal improvements could transform entire regions of the country looked to the East, where the Erie Canal, championed by New York State Governor Dewitt Clinton, was completed in 1825. The 365-mile-long waterway accelerated the delivery of goods between the Great Lakes and New York City, created a new era of prosperity for towns along its path and gave New York a new nickname: the Empire State*

1837-54
Illinois Lawyer

The Springfield Years

On April 15, 1837, Illinois state legislator Abraham Lincoln, 28, moved from New Salem to Springfield, Ill., seat of Sangamon County, where he hung up his shingle to begin practicing law with an admiring mentor. In the years to come, Lincoln would put down deep roots in this city, whose future he had helped secure when he led the recent effort to make it the new capital of Illinois.

During these Springfield years, Lincoln married a Kentucky-born woman who was his superior on the social scale. He suffered a severe mental breakdown, the second of his life. He bought a home and became a father. He completed the last of four two-year terms in the Illinois legislature, and he served a single term in the U.S. House of Representatives, where he took a strong stand against a popular President's popular war, putting him at odds with his friends and constituents. He grew in his mastery of the law, settling into a busy practice with a younger partner, his future biographer, and riding the circuit of Illinois county seats to try small-town cases.

His political career was behind him, it seemed. "From 1849 to 1854, both inclusive, [I] practiced law more assiduously than ever before," he later wrote. The self-educated country boy had transformed himself into a respected, citified attorney. But the notion that he would one day ascend to become the leader of his nation would have seemed a fantasy to those who knew him, as well as to Abraham Lincoln, Illinois lawyer.

First digs *When Lincoln moved to Springfield in 1837, he lived in a general store run by A.Y. Ellis on the west side of the courthouse square. The street is shown here in an 1858 photo; there are no photos of Springfield in 1837, but the town would have been substantially less developed at that time*

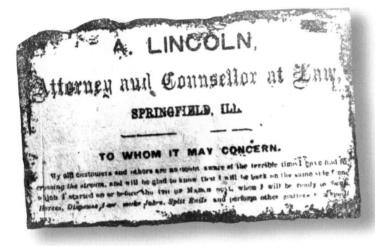

Verdict: A Natural Lawyer

As Abe Lincoln entered his mid-20s, he found himself increasingly drawn to the practice of law. The profession suited his rigorous, rationalizing intellect, his love of books and study, his keen interest in ethics and justice and his flair for argument. It was also a good fit for his unaffected, homespun demeanor, which made him a sympathetic counselor to clients and a convincing advocate to juries.

At that time and in that place, it was a short step for one who made laws to become a practitioner of law. In frontier states like Illinois, most attorneys came to the bar not through law school but by educating themselves in an apprentice system in which they "read law" with a senior mentor and helped prepare cases until they were ready to hang out their own shingle. Lincoln had his first brush with a courtroom when he served as a witness in two cases and as a juror in three more in Springfield, the Sangamon County seat, early in the 1830s. Strongly encouraged by John Todd Stuart, a Springfield lawyer he met in the Black Hawk War (and cousin of his future wife), Lincoln began reading Blackstone's *Commentaries* during his first term in the Illinois legislature. After Lincoln led the successful effort to move the Illinois capital to Springfield, Stuart asked Lincoln to join him as a partner there.

In the 23 years he practiced law before becoming President, Lincoln handled all sorts of cases, and his clients ranged from small-town citizens to national railroad lines. Lincoln took particular delight in riding the circuit of Illinois county seats with a passel of fellow lawyers and judges, either on horseback or driving a horse and buggy. It was a demanding life that took him away from his family for long stretches at a time, but he loved the camaraderie and stories shared at night among this traveling party of talkative, politically minded jurists.

Plain and simple *Above, the law office of Lincoln & Herndon in Springfield was sketched in 1860, after Lincoln was elected President. Sparsely furnished and generally in dire need of a cleaning, it was also badly organized: Lincoln kept current cases in a chaotic stack of papers on his desk. At top left is Lincoln's business card, and below are some of the books he kept in his office*

Mentor, Partner, Biographer

Lincoln's first law partner was a mentor he met in the Black Hawk War, John Todd Stuart. After Lincoln joined him in 1837, Stuart introduced him to the most prominent among Springfield's some 1,500 residents. Lincoln remained Stuart's partner until 1841, when he became junior partner to another leading Springfield attorney, Stephen Logan. Nine years older than Lincoln and a fine litigator, Logan helped Lincoln become a much

John Todd Stuart   **Stephen Logan**

more adept lawyer. A young cousin of several of Lincoln's friends from New Salem days, William (Billy) Herndon, was reading law in the firm. In 1844, when Logan decided to go into partnership with his son, Lincoln set up his own firm and invited Herndon to join him.

William Herndon, in later years

   Herndon happily agreed, and for the next 16 years the hard-drinking abolitionist was Lincoln's partner and closest confidant. After Lincoln's death, Herndon was appalled by the hagiography surrounding his late partner and decided to write an authentic account of his life. For years he traveled Midwestern backroads and corresponded with Lincoln's earliest friends, collecting invaluable memories. Yet he had trouble in committing them to paper, and he finally hired a ghostwriter, Jesse Weik, who primarily wrote the revelatory work finally published in 1889, *Herndon's Lincoln: The True Story of a Great Life.* But Weik never met Lincoln and thus was writing about events that took place decades in the past while relying on the recollections of sources whose memories were fallible. Result: *Herndon's Lincoln* is both our best account of Lincoln's life—and a puzzle that keeps historians in clover, arguing over facts, character portrayals and the personal and political biases of Herndon, Weik and their sources with an ardor Lincoln the lawyer might admire.

43

Religion

A Rough-Hewn Spiritual Life

As a child of frontier America in the first half of the 19th century, Abe Lincoln was raised in a society saturated in the Bible and attuned to the voice of the preacher. In this age of the Second Great Awakening, Protestant Evangelists gathered in enormous camp meetings to take part in revivals that lasted for days—and which also served as homecomings, family reunions, trade fairs and occasions for courtship. No doubt some of the first debates young Abe heard involved the merits of religious denominations rather than political parties. Lincoln's parents were Baptists of a strong Calvinist stripe; this fatalistic faith and its stern God of iron justice and unknowable motives would stay with Lincoln all his life. He would often quote *Hamlet:* "There's a divinity that shapes our ends/ Rough-hew them how we will."

Even so, Lincoln's mind was not made for the pieties of religion; he always argued for the primacy of reason over feeling. As he recalled, the one time his father grew angry at him was when he caught Abe mocking the frantic exertions of a backwoods preacher for friends. As he grew older, Lincoln became a free-thinker who, according to close friend William Herndon, joined other young men in questioning the divinity of Christ and lampooning organized religion. A favorite book was Thomas Paine's *The Age of Reason*, a tract aimed like a bullet at the tenets of organized religion.

But this youthful scoffer would learn to acknowledge a higher power, for Lincoln's spiritual life underwent a powerful evolution as he grew older, though he never joined a denomination and was not a church-goer. He had always loved the Bible, if perhaps more for its wealth of wonderful stories and characters rather than its message of Christian salvation. As President, he kept a Bible on his desk at all times. But in his writings and speeches of the 1850s and '60s, Lincoln increasingly expresses a sense that our lives are not ours to control but rather are shaped by a divine will to which we must learn to submit. This was a deeply fatalistic form of faith, perhaps informed by the sorrows he felt as two of his children died, and as he seemed to assume the full weight of the scores of thousands of lives lost in the Civil War. His writings in the war years reveal a man seeking to justify the ways of a God who resembles the towering Lord of the patriarchs rather than the loving Christ of the New Testament.

Lincoln's God is the majestic, law-giving God of Isaiah, the "wonderful counsellor." It is perhaps not a coincidence that those seeking a visual corollary for this stern, august, unreachable deity might find it in the nation's capital, in the magnificent seated statue of the 16th President created by sculptor Daniel Chester French for the Lincoln Memorial.

Fundamentals *Above, an evangelistic camp meeting of the mid-1800s attracts a host of believers. Left, a 19th century Bible; Lincoln was steeped from youth in its stories and characters*

WHAT LINCOLN SAID

"If we shall suppose that American slavery is one of those offenses which, in the providence of God, must needs come, but which, having continued through His appointed time, He now wills to remove, and that He gives to both North and South this terrible war as the woe due to those by whom the offense came, shall we discern therein any departure from those divine attributes which the believers in a living God always ascribe to him?" —SECOND INAUGURAL ADDRESS

Knight of the Woeful Countenance

Abe Lincoln was a mercurial figure who could be a boisterous, storytelling extrovert at one moment and a gloomy, haunted introvert the next. He was a *character,* in the sense people used the word in his time and ours: a larger-than-life figure who enthralled those he met with his unlikely mixture of signature traits. Within his awkward, towering frame there was room to accommodate a backwoods jester with a taste for outhouse humor, a brilliant lawyer with an unrivaled flair for close analysis, a compelling orator who could move audiences to tears, a masterly politician with a shrewd eye for the public mood, and a gloomy, miserable loner who suffered from the "hypo," his term for his bouts of depression and despair.

It's that last figure who has come into sharper focus in recent years, thanks to Joshua Wolf Shenk's revelatory 2005 book *Lincoln's Melancholy.* Shenk constructs a compelling portrait of a Lincoln who suffered through two severe, near suicidal, attacks of depression in his life and whose strongly saturnine disposition was familiar to all who knew him well.

If there is a Lincoln who eludes our grasp in recent years, it's the rawboned storyteller whose taste for corny, ribald jokes seems utterly at odds with the marble monument we've made of him. Lincoln's gifts as a raconteur were so renowned that when ex-President Martin van Buren (a Jackson man, no less) was passing through Illinois in 1842, local boosters demanded that he spend time with Lincoln, the best storyteller in the state. Abe regaled the New Yorker for hours, we're told, reducing him to tears of laughter. In later years, however, Easterners unprepared for Abe's homely yarns would deride him as a country-fried simpleton.

Lincoln's voice also escapes us: contemporaries tell us its timbre was high-pitched, even shrill. Thanks to the advancing technology of his time, we're fortunate to have photographs of Lincoln (Washington and Jefferson we know only through paintings and drawings). But photo subjects in his day were ordered to remain still during the long exposure process, so we'll never know the animated Lincoln described by aide John Nicolay: "… a face that moved through a thousand delicate gradations of line and contour, light and shade, sparkle of the eye and curve of the lip … There are many pictures of Lincoln; there is no portrait of him."

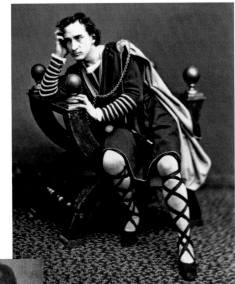

Favorites *The portrait on the left page is the first photo we have of Lincoln; it was taken in 1846, the year he was elected to Congress, in Springfield. Above is Edwin Booth, the greatest Shakespearean actor of Lincoln's day (and brother of his assassin); at left is Robert Burns and below is Edgar Allan Poe*

Lincoln's Reading List

From his bibliophilic boyhood to the last hours of his life, Lincoln was a reader. When he found himself in charge of a Union army whose generals seemed as clueless as their Commander in Chief, he knew just what to do: he went to the Library of Congress, checked out books on military strategy and began to educate himself.

Lincoln loved books that spoke in parables and fables, all grist for his apt political and judicial anecdotes. He was a great student of the Bible and is said to have memorized Aesop's *Fables* as a lad. In later years he delighted in the vernacular political satire of "Petroleum V. Nasby" (David R. Locke) and "Orpheus C. Kerr" (Robert H. Newell). He was immune to the leisurely attractions of fiction, apparently; an early attempt to read Walter Scott was a failure. Instead, his ear for the spoken word led him to poetry; he loved Robert Burns, and he was a great fan of the morose Edgar Allan Poe, whose *The Raven* he knew by heart. Above all he preferred Shakespeare, whom he first encountered in his youth. He could quote large portions of the plays; *Macbeth,* the haunted play of corrupting power, was his favorite. In his melancholy mode, his favored poem was a saccharine, humbling meditation on man's frailty by the Scot William Knox, *Mortality.* Its first line and theme: "Oh! Why should the spirit of mortal be proud!"

A Surprising, Enduring Union

The awkward, lanky bumpkin approached the sophisti-cated rich girl at a ball in Springfield, Ill., in December 1839. "Miss Todd," he said, "I want to dance with you in the worst way." Thus began a courtship that was a study in contrasts: Mary Todd, 21, was educated; Abraham Lincoln, 30, was barely schooled. She came from a rich, slaveholding family; he was from backwoods poverty. But they also had much in common: born in Kentucky and later transplanted to Illinois, they had both lost their mothers at a young age. Both were fascinated by politics, and, above all else, both were ambitious.

After moving to the home of her married sister Elizabeth Edwards on Springfield's "Aristocracy Hill" (in part because the ratio of suitable women to eligible bachelors was far more encouraging in Springfield than in Lexington, Ky.), the blue-eyed, charming Todd allowed herself to be wooed only by young politicians. Lincoln's future rival, Stephen A. Douglas, was among her suitors. Soon, however, she was engaged to the rawboned young lawyer and state legislator she had met at the dance, much to the distress of her upscale relatives, who felt that the awkward Lincoln was beneath her.

The Todd family's concerns seemed confirmed when Lincoln broke off the engagement shortly before the appointed wedding day, Jan. 1, 1841. Lincoln's friend and biographer William Herndon claims that the future President jilted his fiancée on the wedding day itself, but this account has largely been discredited by historians. (Herndon and Mary Todd detested each other.) Today, most historians believe that Lincoln was suffering cold feet, perhaps brought on by relentless snubs from Todd's family; others think another belle had turned his head.

Whatever the cause, Lincoln, who regarded his integrity as "the chief gem of my character," felt that he had behaved dishonorably; for him, no sin could be worse. For the second time, a romance cut short led to a mental breakdown so complete that friends feared he might take his life. He wrote to his good friend Joshua Speed, "I am now the most miserable man living. If what I feel were equally distributed to the whole human family there would not be one cheerful face on the earth."

But within a year, friends had intervened to broker a reconciliation. The wife of the editor of the Sangamo *Journal* arranged to have Todd and Lincoln run into each other "unexpectedly" in her home. Soon, they were meeting regularly (and secretly) there. On the morning of Nov. 4, 1842, Lincoln, now 33, barged in on Charles Dresser, the local Episcopal minister (and Todd's brother-in-law) at breakfast and blurted out, "I want to get hitched tonight." In a hastily-arranged ceremony that evening, the groom handed Todd a ring inscribed with the words LOVE IS ETERNAL.

Mrs. Lincoln's sights perhaps did not extend so far into the future. When friends asked why she had married so far beneath her station, Mary answered matter-of-factly: "He is to be President of the United States someday. If I had not thought so I never would have married him, for you can see he is not pretty."

Southern belle *Mary Todd Lincoln in the first photograph we have of her, taken circa 1846*

A Healing Sojourn in Kentucky

After breaking off his engagement to Mary Todd, a deeply depressed Lincoln turned for comfort to his closest friend, Joshua Speed, a Kentuckian of about Abe's age. Speed was a shopkeeper, above whose store the two had lived, along with several other young men, from the time Lincoln first arrived in Springfield four years before. Speed was gravely concerned; he feared Lincoln might attempt suicide and decided "to remove razors from his room—take away all knives and other such dangerous things." When Speed's father, a wealthy, slave-owning farmer, died in 1841, the young man returned to Kentucky, intent on settling down with his own fiancée. In August, a still brooding, unsettled Lincoln accepted an invitation to visit the Speed plantation in Farmington, where, for six weeks, he rested and healed.

Speed in later years

The trip also fostered Lincoln's political education. The Speeds were slave owners as well as moderate abolitionists, who had tried, unsuccessfully, to persuade their black farmhands to return to Africa. Observing the family's moral anguish helped cement Lincoln's increasing sense that slavery was a curse on both its victims and its perpetrators. On their return to Illinois, he and Speed traveled the Ohio River in a boat that also carried a dozen manacled slaves. "That sight was a continual torment to me," he would recall later.

The sojourn in Kentucky helped Lincoln right himself emotionally. Asked by Speed a decade later why he had never fulfilled the worst fears of his friends by ending his own life, Lincoln replied that he could not bear to leave the world without having done anything to make other human beings remember that he had lived. "I have an irrepressible desire to live," he explained, "until I can be assured that the world is a little better for my having lived in it."

The Speed home in Farmington

Settling Down

For Mary Todd Lincoln, marriage was a step down in the world. Immediately after their wedding at the elegant home of sister Elizabeth Edwards and her husband Ninian, the bride and groom were driven by carriage to their new lodgings: the Globe Tavern, a boarding house and saloon. Here the Lincolns rented a single 8-ft. by 14-ft. room for $4 per week, taking meals with their fellow boarders. While it was not unusual for young couples to begin their married lives in such circumstances, it is a testimony to Mary Todd Lincoln's firm belief in her husband's future that she was willing to accept such a steep (and public) decline in her personal circumstances: the Globe was a long way from both the Todd family home in Kentucky and the Edwards home on Springfield's "Aristocracy Hill." Mary's sisters, it appears, now began to snub her.

But Lincoln was increasingly successful, and his wife's ambition helped fire his own. Shortly after their first son, Robert, was born at the Globe in August 1843, the Lincolns signed a contract with the Rev. Charles Dresser, the minister who had married them, to purchase a wood-frame house at Eighth and Jackson streets. The price was $1,500; the Lincoln family marked time in a small rented house nearby for a few months before moving into their new home in May 1844. They began remodeling and adding rooms in 1846, a process that would be repeated five times in the years to come.

Here the Lincolns settled into what seems to have been a reasonably happy family life. The principal strains on the young family involved Lincoln's work as a circuit-riding attorney, which kept him away from home for weeks at a time, and Mary's tendency to fly off the handle when flustered. This was the only home the Lincolns would ever own, but they did occupy a larger dwelling from 1861-65. One suspects Mary may have enjoyed welcoming her sisters to the White House.

A Study in Sorrow

Of the Lincolns' four sons, only one—the eldest, Robert Todd Lincoln—lived to maturity. Second son Edward, right, was born in 1846 and died in 1850, not yet 4. After Eddie's death, the Lincolns quickly had two more sons, Willie and Thomas, shown below with Mary in 1860.

William Wallace Lincoln, born in 1850, died in 1862; some believe he was Lincoln's favorite child, and his death left his parents in deep grief. Thomas, or "Tad," was born in 1853 and his parents spoiled him, perhaps because he had a slight speech impediment. His death at 18, in 1871, sent his mother into a decline from which she never recovered. Robert Lincoln died at 82 in 1926, three years after he helped dedicate the Lincoln Memorial.

Formerly humble *There are no photos of the Lincoln home as it appeared in 1844, when the couple first moved in. That was a modest, three-room cottage; the picture above shows the home in its final form, following several additions and renovations. The most extensive alterations took place in 1855, when an entire second story was added to the building.*

The photograph above, taken in 1860, shows Lincoln and son Willie on the front porch of the family home, where the nameplate above hung. Son Tad is peeking out from behind a fence post, but is difficult to see.

"When the conduct of men is designed to be influenced, persuasion, *kind, unassuming persuasion, should ever be adopted. It is an old and a true maxim, that 'a drop of honey catches more flies than a gallon of gall.'"*

A larger arena *When Abe and Mary Lincoln arrived in Washington, D.C., in 1847, the U.S. Capitol still was topped by a temporary dome, above. This circa 1846 picture, the earliest known photograph of the building, shows it as they would have seen it. Work on the building and its final dome continued during his presidency*

Mr. Lincoln Goes to Washington

Lincoln's second term in the Illinois legislature concluded in a double triumph for his "Long Nine" group: the state capital was moved to Springfield, and the vast plan of public works to be financed by state debt and supported by the group was approved. But the nationwide financial collapse that soon followed, known to history as the Panic of 1837, ensured the plan's failure.

Yet Lincoln was still a popular public servant, and when he was elected to a third term in 1838, he hoped to become speaker of the house. He failed, but continued to serve in the important post of floor leader for the Whig minority. His new role landed him in a farcical event in December 1840 that would amuse Illinois politicians for years. The Whigs, supporting the Illinois State Bank that Democrats strongly opposed, were attempting to keep the legislature in session to prevent the bank from bankruptcy, while the Democrats needed to adjourn the session to kill off the institution. At a moment of crisis, the Democrats locked the door of the assembly room to keep Lincoln and a few fellow Whigs inside, thus forming a quorum for adjournment. But the Whigs, led by Lincoln, escaped by leaping out a second-floor window. He always referred to this inglorious self-defenestration as "the jumping scrape."

Lincoln was elected for a fourth term in the legislature in August 1840, and that summer and fall he campaigned for Whig presidential candidate William Henry Harrison, traveling across Illinois to speak in favor of "Tippecanoe and Tyler too." The campaign ended in victory for the Whigs, but within a month of his inauguration, Harrison died, and John Tyler proved a disappointing President for the Whigs.

Lincoln's fourth term would be his last as a state legislator. His marriage to Mary Todd, with all its personal complications, and his subsequent need to build up his fledgling law practice, kept him from seeking re-election in 1842. But there was another reason for his decision: he was beginning to consider running for a seat in the U.S. Congress, representing Illinois' newly formed Seventh Congressional District. John Todd Stuart, his onetime law partner, had occupied the seat for two terms, prior to its redistricting, but was now stepping down. And the district tilted to the Whigs. But Lincoln failed to win the party's nomination, which went to his good friend Edward A. Baker— ironically, the namesake of Lincoln's second son. A good party man, Lincoln supported Baker's successful campaign for the post, putting himself in line to succeed him, for Baker had agreed to serve only a single term in Washington. Just as he had hoped, Lincoln was elected to succeed Baker on Aug. 3, 1846.

Mr. Lincoln was going to Washington—although, due to the slow pace of traveling in the period, his first session did not begin until December 1847, more than a year after his election. When he arrived in the nation's capital, he was not alone: defying the custom of the time, his wife Mary accompanied him. Always ambitious for his success, she was eager for the couple to make their mark in Washington. As it turned out, she would not attend all the sessions at which Lincoln served, which may have been just as well: as a freshman, Lincoln made no great mark in the House of Representatives, though he was diligent in attendance and eagerly took the measure of his fellow Congressmen, forming acquaintances that would serve him in the presidency. His first term in Congress would be his last, for Lincoln took a strong stand against the U.S. war with Mexico, a decision that made him deeply unpopular with voters and would keep him out of the political arena for six years.

A Voice of Dissent Against a Popular Conflict

When Lincoln ran for a seat in the U.S. House of Representatives in 1846, he promised his constituents that he would only serve a single term in Congress. Not to worry: by the end of his term, Lincoln had made himself so deeply unpopular with Illinois voters that his self-imposed term limit proved to be a blessing, allowing him to escape certain defeat had he mounted a bid for re-election.

As it happened, President James K. Polk also came into office vowing to serve only a single term, and he kept his promise. But in four years, he achieved much. His successful war with Mexico, if suspicious in origin, was impressive in military execution and rich in rewards: at the end of the 22-month conflict, Mexico signed over to the U.S. the land now occupied by California, Nevada and Utah, as well as portions of Colorado, Arizona, New Mexico and Wyoming. A nation in the thrall of Manifest Destiny cheered Polk and war heroes Winfield Scott and Zachary Taylor.

But Lincoln and many other Whigs believed Polk had started a war of aggression based on a lie. On two critical occasions, Lincoln rose in the House to question Polk's veracity, asking him to prove that the Mexicans had crossed national borders to draw first blood on U.S. soil in the conflict, as Polk had claimed. Flush with victory, Polk simply paid no heed to the small-fry Illinois Congressman—nor did national newspapers, to the ambitious Lincoln's regret. But his constituents, including law partner, close friend and fellow Whig William Herndon, found Lincoln's behavior unpatriotic. His stand, said Herndon, "sealed Lincoln's doom as a Congressman."

War heroes *The U.S. campaign in Mexico was conducted with brisk efficiency. It bred war-hero President Zachary Taylor and served as a training ground for many of the future military commanders of the Civil War. At the Sept. 12-13, 1847, Battle of Chapultepec outside Mexico City, above, the first American over the citadel wall was Lieutenant George Pickett, who would lead the Southern charge at Gettysburg.*

At top right is a picture of U.S. troops in Saltillo; it is believed to be the first war photograph ever taken. Another innovation, the telegraph, kept Americans abreast of events. At near right is Polk, the expansionist President who also signed a treaty with Britain that brought the land that would become Oregon, Idaho and Washington State into the Union.

WHAT LINCOLN SAID

"Let the President [Polk] answer the interrogatories I proposed ... Let him answer fully, fairly, candidly. Let him answer with facts, and not with arguments. Let him remember, he sits where Washington sat; and so remembering, let him answer as Washington would answer ... so let him attempt no evasion, no equivocation."

1854-60
National Stage

A New Sense of Urgency

When Abraham Lincoln returned to Illinois from Washington, D.C., he thought he had put politics behind him. The increasingly successful lawyer anticipated a life of quiet prosperity, far from the national stage. But it was not to be: as he tells us in his brief 1860 autobiography, "From 1849 to 1854, both inclusive, [I] practiced law more assiduously than ever before ... I was losing interest in politics, when the repeal of the Missouri Compromise aroused me again."

The man behind what Lincoln chose to call the repeal of the Missouri Compromise was his old nemesis, Illinois Senator Stephen A. Douglas, whose Kansas-Nebraska Act of 1854 put the burning issue of slavery's future back on the nation's front pages. America's reckoning over human bondage had been delayed several times, most significantly by the Missouri Compromise of 1820 and again by the Compromise of 1850. The first applied to states formed from the Louisiana Purchase and banned slavery above an east-west line line formed by the southern boundary of Missouri. The second balanced slave and free states in the far West and included a fugitive slave law that made it easier for Southern owners to recover slaves who had escaped to the North.

The Kansas-Nebraska Act, violating the spirit of the 1850 accord, declared that the voters of each territory, rather than the U.S. government, had the right to determine whether it should be slave or free. Douglas called this principle "popular sovereignty." But Lincoln denounced the Act; roused into action, he returned to the political arena and began a crusade against slavery's extension that would take him to the presidency, civil war and a martyr's death.

Clashing colors *This 1856 map reveals a nation deeply divided by slavery and geography. Free states of the North, and California, are pink; Southern slave states are brown; territories in the process of being settled, incipient states, are green. It was the future of this last group that would bring civil war*

The Peculiar Institution

Thomas Jefferson, the slaveholder who wrote the ringing words "We hold these truths to be self-evident: that all men are created equal," understood that in accepting human bondage, the U.S. was making a bargain with the devil, one that would force an eventual crisis. "We have the wolf by the ears; and we can neither hold him, nor safely let him go. Justice is in one scale, and self-preservation in the other," he wrote in 1820, as the nation was arguing over the extension of slavery into new territories. The Missouri Compromise of 1820 resolved some issues of slavery's extension, but it simply put off the looming confrontation with the wolf of bondage for another day.

By the 1850s, that day was coming closer. The cries for justice Jefferson anticipated were ringing louder than ever before. The ranks of Abolitionists were swelling, as Northerners aroused by the Fugitive Slave Act of 1850 came face to face with the brutalities of bondage, watching slave-catchers march manacled blacks through their cities. Yet the calls for self-preservation in the South were just as loud: King Cotton had woven a straitjacket around the Southern planters, binding them to an economy that, they fervently argued, could only exist based on the cheap toil of the slaves.

When Lincoln returned to politics in 1854, roughly 1 of every 8 Americans was a black slave. Lincoln detested slavery all his life, but before the war he did not join the Northern Abolitionists, whom he found extreme, self-righteous and unrealistic in underestimating the difficulties that would ensue if slavery were abolished. Instead, he strongly opposed slavery's extension and, alone among major politicians, refused to label slavery a Southern problem; he described it as every American's problem.

Bondage *Above left, slaves on Port Royal Island, S.C.; at top right, slaves grind sugar in Georgia. The importing of slaves from Africa into the U.S. was outlawed in 1808, but the black population was so well established in the South that it continued to grow. In the years before the Civil War, many Southern whites lived in fear of an uprising by their slaves, who vastly outnumbered them in many areas*

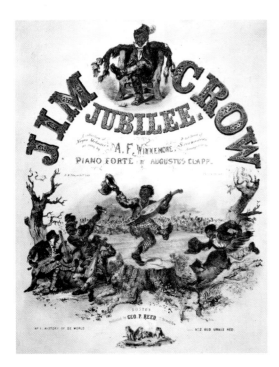

Lincoln and Racism

The complex interplay between whites and blacks in America found one of its most unusual expressions in the most popular entertainment form of Lincoln's day, the minstrel show, left. Beginning in the 1830s, it swept across the nation, the most vital and certainly most revealing art form of its time. With white entertainers performing in blackface, the minstrel show reflected the deep racism that pervaded U.S. life at the time, even as it expressed the white culture's exhilarating embrace of black culture, a love that could only speak its name, it seems, in disguise.

Lincoln's hatred of slavery ran so deep, he claimed, that he could not remember a time when he did not feel it. But we must not confuse his moral vision with his racial vision. Far from sharing the color-blind ideals of our time, Lincoln held many of the racist attitudes of his, and these prejudices were not reserved to blacks; he derided Mexicans as "greasers." In fact, Lincoln had little contact with black Americans, either slave or free, before he became President: he had no close friends who were black in Illinois, and his few contacts with slavery involved visits to the Speed and Todd homes in Kentucky, where bondage was practiced in a paternalistic fashion. For Lincoln, as well as for the nation, the crises of the Civil War era would offer an opportunity to view black Americans with fresh, and much more appreciative, eyes.

Caught in a Web of Bondage

The map at right reveals how deeply slavery was woven into the fabric of America in Lincoln's time. It's an eye-opener, for, from the vantage point of the 21st century, slavery is often viewed simply as a moral issue involving human rights, in which those who supported the practice were clearly in the wrong.

And they were. But to Americans of Lincoln's time, slavery and its possible abolition involved a wider, more complex range of questions—involving economics, demographics, race and culture—that seemed insoluble. How was the agrarian South to survive economically with no slaves to work the fields? If the 4 million slaves in Southern states were to be set free, where would they live, and what work would they do? Should they remain in America or be sent abroad? And given the racist attitudes of the time, in both North and South, could whites and freed blacks ever live together in harmony?

Lincoln grappled with such issues throughout his political career. As a U.S. Congressman, he proposed a bill that called for a referendum among citizens of the District of Columbia to approve a plan under which slave owners would be paid full value to free their slaves. It met with so little favor that he never introduced the bill. Another of his schemes for dealing with the effects of slavery seems less plausible to modern ears. Throughout his career, well into his presidency, Lincoln supported programs that would send freed blacks to Liberia in Africa or to Central America, where, he argued, they could begin life over again. A few freed slaves were indeed sent abroad under such schemes, but in truth most such plans, like most of the slaves, went nowhere.

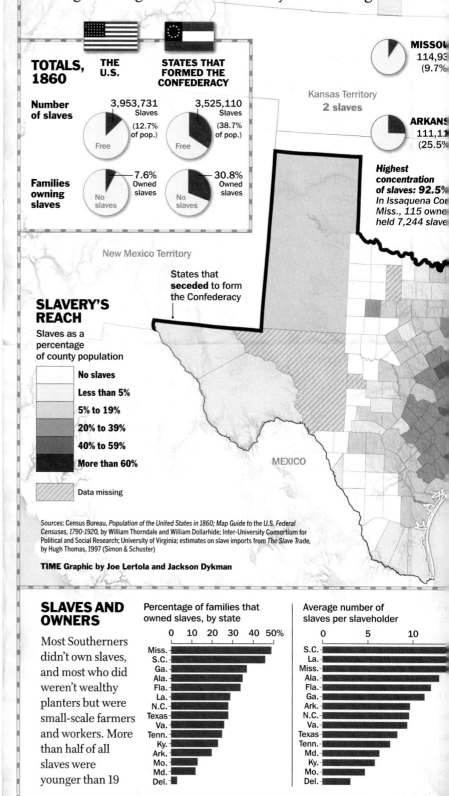

Slavery Up Close

On the eve of the Civil War, 4 million people were held in bondage, fueling the South's economy but cleaving the nation

Nebra
Territ
15 sla

TOTALS, 1860	THE U.S.	STATES THAT FORMED THE CONFEDERACY
Number of slaves	3,953,731 Slaves (12.7% of pop.) Free	3,525,110 Slaves (38.7% of pop.) Free
Families owning slaves	7.6% Owned slaves No slaves	30.8% Owned slaves No slaves

MISSOU
114,93
(9.7%

Kansas Territory
2 slaves

ARKANS
111,11
(25.5%

Highest concentration of slaves: 92.5%
In Issaquena Cou
Miss., 115 owne
held 7,244 slave

New Mexico Territory

States that **seceded** to form the Confederacy

SLAVERY'S REACH

Slaves as a percentage of county population

- No slaves
- Less than 5%
- 5% to 19%
- 20% to 39%
- 40% to 59%
- More than 60%

- Data missing

MEXICO

Sources: Census Bureau, *Population of the United States in 1860*; *Map Guide to the U.S. Federal Censuses, 1790-1920*, by William Thorndale and William Dollarhide; Inter-University Consortium for Political and Social Research; University of Virginia; estimates on slave imports from *The Slave Trade*, by Hugh Thomas, 1997 (Simon & Schuster)

TIME Graphic by Joe Lertola and Jackson Dykman

SLAVES AND OWNERS

Most Southerners didn't own slaves, and most who did weren't wealthy planters but were small-scale farmers and workers. More than half of all slaves were younger than 19

Percentage of families that owned slaves, by state

0   10   20   30   40   50%

Miss.
S.C.
Ga.
Ala.
Fla.
La.
N.C.
Texas
Va.
Tenn.
Ky.
Ark.
Mo.
Md.
Del.

Average number of slaves per slaveholder

0   5   10

S.C.
La.
Miss.
Ala.
Fla.
Ga.
Ark.
N.C.
Va.
Texas
Tenn.
Md.
Ky.
Mo.
Del.

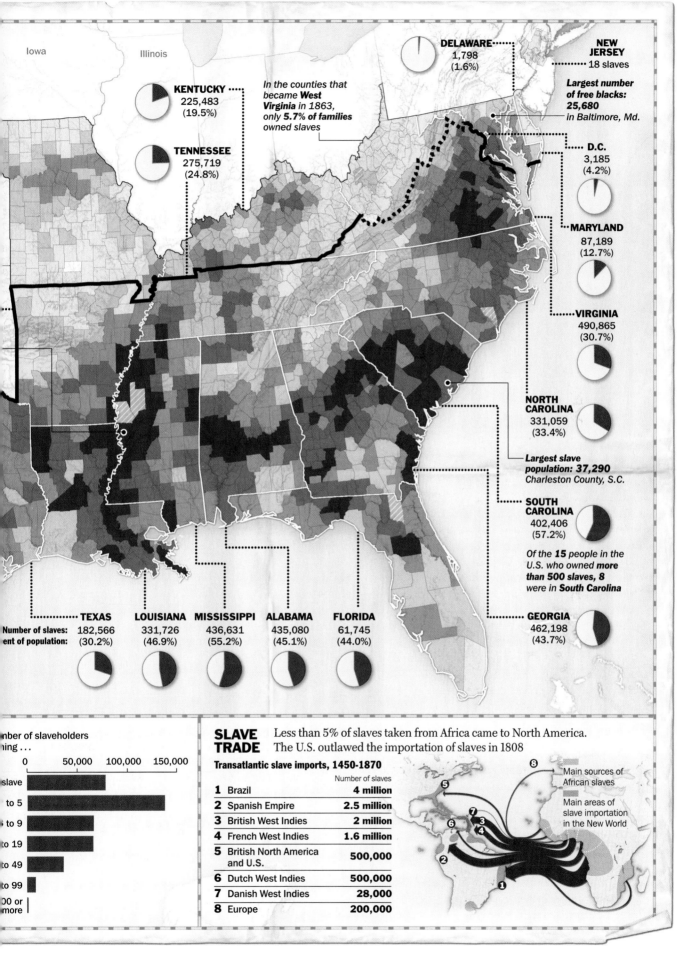

Iowa

Illinois

DELAWARE
1,798
(1.6%)

NEW JERSEY
18 slaves

Largest number of free blacks:
25,680
in Baltimore, Md.

KENTUCKY
225,483
(19.5%)

In the counties that became West Virginia in 1863, only 5.7% of families owned slaves

TENNESSEE
275,719
(24.8%)

D.C.
3,185
(4.2%)

MARYLAND
87,189
(12.7%)

VIRGINIA
490,865
(30.7%)

NORTH CAROLINA
331,059
(33.4%)

Largest slave population: 37,290 Charleston County, S.C.

SOUTH CAROLINA
402,406
(57.2%)

Of the 15 people in the U.S. who owned more than 500 slaves, 8 were in South Carolina

	TEXAS	**LOUISIANA**	**MISSISSIPPI**	**ALABAMA**	**FLORIDA**	**GEORGIA**
Number of slaves:	182,566	331,726	436,631	435,080	61,745	462,198
ent of population:	(30.2%)	(46.9%)	(55.2%)	(45.1%)	(44.0%)	(43.7%)

mber of slaveholders
ning . . .

0	50,000	100,000	150,000

slave

to 5

to 9

to 19

to 49

to 99

00 or
more

SLAVE TRADE

Less than 5% of slaves taken from Africa came to North America.
The U.S. outlawed the importation of slaves in 1808

Transatlantic slave imports, 1450-1870

Number of slaves

		Number of slaves
1	Brazil	**4 million**
2	Spanish Empire	**2.5 million**
3	British West Indies	**2 million**
4	French West Indies	**1.6 million**
5	British North America and U.S.	**500,000**
6	Dutch West Indies	**500,000**
7	Danish West Indies	**28,000**
8	Europe	**200,000**

Main sources of African slaves

Main areas of slave importation in the New World

61

A Divided, Galvanized Nation

Slavery was the dominant American political issue in the late 1840s and '50s, but it was only one among many highly charged social currents that made this period one of the most roisterous and divisive in U.S. history. Massive immigration, women's rights, the Gold Rush, rapid urbanization, the new telegraph that seemed to accelerate the pace of daily events even as it wove the nation into a much tighter network than ever before—all contributed to the sense of a giddy nation careening out of control. It was an age of extremes, and when Abraham Lincoln returned to the political arena in the mid-1850s, he would stand out precisely because of his determined, unswerving moderation. He was sui generis: a nondrinker all his life, he refused to support laws forbidding another man his dram. An active, eloquent opponent of slavery, he chose not to demonize Southerners, while at the other extreme, he firmly opposed the radical Abolitionists. He dreaded mob rule, as exemplified by the Philadelphia men in the illustration above, whose tall beaver hats distinguish them as anti-immigrant nativists. They are shown battling police who are protecting new arrivals in 1844.

By the early 1850s, America's old two-party system was as dead as Andrew Jackson. Reflecting an urgent age, a host of new parties sprouted, each clinging to a single, defining issue. Lincoln's party, the Whigs, would simply wither away, as members deserted it for new, energetic alternatives. Lincoln would soon join them, as he helped found a party that would build a broad new coalition to support progress and fight slavery.

Women Call for the Vote—and Temperance

In an age of social progress, American women began to demand a stronger voice in both family and public life. A group of such progressive women gathered at Seneca Falls, N.Y., in 1848, below, to call for female suffrage. They would get their wish—72 years later. In the meantime, their crusade to improve women's lives shaped the Temperance movement. This powerful political force was not the work of Puritans seeking to remove all pleasure from life, as it is sometimes pictured. Instead, it sought to reduce the widespread incidents of violence visited upon women and children by drunken men and tolerated by a male-dominated society that often preferred to look the other way. Though he would not join this movement, Lincoln admired many of its leaders and shared many of its goals.

Newcomers and Know-Nothings

The pounding pulse of Chicago's Haymarket is almost palpable in the 1860 photo at left. America was rapidly urbanizing in the 1840s and '50s, especially in the North. If the South relied on slaves for cheap labor, the North had its own supply: European immigrants, 5 million of whom arrived in the U.S. between 1815-60. Many were Irish Roman Catholics fleeing the famine that killed 1 million of their countrymen, while German and Polish Catholics flocked to today's Midwest.

Many of these arrivals were unfunded, uneducated and, to American eyes, uncouth. They were thus unwelcome. A strong movement of native-born U.S. Protestants sprang up, devoted to forbidding full rights to the newcomers. The most prominent such group was the Native American Party, a.k.a. the Know-Nothings, so called because its members feigned ignorance of the lodges where they gathered. The group was most influential in the mid-1850s. A sample plank from the party's 1856 platform: "The sending back of all foreign paupers." Know-Nothings flourished where Protestants held sway, including Illinois, and Lincoln was at times suspected of sharing their goals. His thoughts on the matter are below.

WHAT LINCOLN SAID

"I am not a Know-Nothing. That is certain. How could I be? How can any one who abhors the oppression of Negroes, be in favor of degrading classes of white people? Our progress in degeneracy appears to me to be pretty rapid. As a nation, we began by declaring that 'all men are created equal.' We now practically read it 'all men are created equal, except Negroes.' When the Know-Nothings get control, it will read 'all men are created equal, except Negroes and foreigners and Catholics.' When it comes to this, I shall prefer emigrating to some country where they make no pretense of loving liberty—to Russia, for instance, where despotism can be taken pure and without the base alloy of hypocrisy."

Kansas, Nebraska, Lincoln, Douglas

The passage of the Kansas-Nebraska Act in 1854, which decreed that the citizens of U.S. frontier territories could decide for themselves whether their regions should be slave or free, put the nation on a fast track to civil war. Slavery's malicious influence, so long bottled up by the rough balance between Northern and Southern states, now exploded on the frontier.

Although slavery held little appeal for residents of the area that would become Nebraska, Kansas was closely divided between pro-slavery and abolition forces. A miniature civil war soon erupted in which settlers battled one another and dozens were killed. In Illinois, Abraham Lincoln felt he must speak out. After weeks of preparation, he stood before a packed hall in Peoria on Oct. 16, 1854, to argue the merits of the Act with Stephen Douglas, its author. In a magnificent 3-hr. speech, Lincoln denounced slavery and its extension into the territories, invoked the Declaration of Independence to prove that slavery violated its most basic tenets and—to unexpected, brilliant effect—refused to blame the South for slavery's evils and called for all Americans to help redress them now. Breaking with convention, he avoided sarcasm, stuck to the facts and emphasized analytical clarity. In this ringing and carefully argued call to action, the man and the hour had met: the Lincoln of mighty oratory and cleansing vision—the Lincoln of history—was born in Peoria.

F. Beard.

REPUBLICAN MEETING.

Those who are in favor of **KANSAS** being a *Free State*, and who disapprove of the outrages committed in that Territory; and who are opposed to the Extension of Slavery, and who disapprove of the Repeal of the Missouri Compromise, are invited to attend a **MEETING** to be held *in Church's Hall* in the Village of Roslyn, on **Tuesday**, the 26th inst., at 7 P. M.

Ladies are invited to attend.

Parke Godwin

W. C. Bryant.

Gideon Frost

Roslyn, August 21st, 1856.

"Bloody Kansas" *Would the growing territory of Kansas be slave or free? The Kansas-Nebraska Act put that question in the hands of its settlers. But the issue was so contentious that a gruesome guerrilla war broke out between pro- and anti-slavery factions. Nearby Missouri was a slave state, and armed bands of raiders began crossing the border to intimidate "free-soil" settlers who opposed slavery. On the left page, five such settlers were killed by a pro-slavery group from Missouri near the Marais des Cygnes River on May 19, 1858.*

Slavery supporters from Missouri—some of them bribed by dollars and whiskey—also crossed into Kansas to cast illegal votes for slavery in the territory, shown above. At left is a poster for an anti-slavery meeting.

JOHN C. FREMONT. THE REPUBLICANS CHOICE FOR PRESIDENT

AND

WM. L. DAYTON. VICE PRESIDENT FROM 1857 TO 1861

Trailblazers *The first Republican national convention was held in Philadelphia in June 1856, where delegates passed over such front-runners as Senator William H. Seward of New York (later Lincoln's Secretary of State) and chose the flamboyant Western explorer John C. Frémont as their candidate. The Illinois delegation arranged to have Lincoln nominated for Vice President—it was his debut on the national political stage— but he lost the vote, 253-110, to the former New Jersey Senator William L. Dayton.*

Reflecting the era's shifting political tides, Frémont ran against two candidates: the Democrats ran James Buchanan and the new American Party, a nativist group linked to the Know-Nothings, ran Millard Fillmore. Lincoln stumped Illinois giving speeches for Frémont, but Buchanan won.

Grand New Party

All his life, according to Abe Lincoln, he was a Whig in politics. As they coalesced into a major party in the 1830s, the Whigs stood for certain unifying principles—a high tariff, government investment for internal improvements, an active federal legislature, opposition to slavery. But they could be defined as much by what they stood against as what they stood for: they were the anti-Jackson party. Now, in the headlong rush of the 1850s, both Jackson's Democratic Party and Henry Clay's Whig Party would be shattered. The Democrats began to divide along territorial lines, into Southern and Northern branches. The Whigs, in contrast, simply ran out of steam as voters deserted their coalition in favor of more robust new ones.

In the elections of 1840 and 1848, the Whigs nominated war heroes for the presidency and enjoyed success. But the 1840 victor, Indian-fighter William Henry Harrison, died a month after taking office—and, incredibly enough, Zachary Taylor, the Mexican War hero elected in 1848, also died in office. His successor, Millard Fillmore, was the last Whig President: by agreeing to passage of the Fugitive Slave Act as part of the

Compromise of 1850, he effectively split the party, most of whose members despised the act. In the 1852 election, Democrat Franklin Pierce defeated the last Whig presidential candidate, General Winfield Scott, yet another war hero.

A new party soon arose from the ashes of Whig ruin: the Republican Party. Founded in Jackson, Mich., in 1854 by opponents of the Kansas-Nebraska Act, it would eventually attract Whigs, Free Soilers and Know-Nothings to its banner. Some Republicans opposed slavery's extension but not its existence, while others called for outright abolition. But all stood for progress: urbanization, new technologies, free homesteads for farmers. The party's first presidential candidate, above, was the noted Western explorer John C. Frémont, who lost to Democrat James Buchanan in 1856. Sizing up the new group at the very first Republican meeting in Illinois in 1856, which was composed primarily of journalists, was the noted attorney Abraham Lincoln. He liked what he saw, and he soon became a leading Republican in both his home state and around the country.

Just the facts *The portrait at left, a rare image of Lincoln in a white suit rather than his usual dark garb, was taken in 1858, only hours after Lincoln won his most famous law case.*

Lincoln was defending William (Duff) Armstrong, the son of an old friend from New Salem, who was charged with being an accessory in a murder trial. The state's key witness claimed he had seen Armstrong strike the victim in the face with a slingshot while another man struck him a deadly blow on the back of the head.

In his cross-examination, Lincoln carefully established, without drawing attention to his real intent, that the witness had been able to see the attack from a distance only because of the light shed by the night's full moon. He then triumphantly produced an almanac to prove that the moon had already set at the time of the murder, and Armstrong went free.

Growing Family, Growing Firm

If the subject of this book seems to have disappeared from its pages for a spell, well, that's the idea. After his single term in Washington, Lincoln returned to Springfield to focus on his career and family, putting the political arena behind him. It was at this time—on Feb. 1, 1850—that the Lincolns' second son, Eddie, not yet 4, died of tuberculosis. His parents were shattered. But Mary was soon pregnant again, and son Willie, born late in 1850, was followed by another son, Thomas, or "Tad" (for "Tadpole"), in 1853. Lincoln was more prosperous than ever before—the firm of Lincoln & Herndon was now representing large railroad companies—and he and Mary, who possessed Todd family funds of her own, were able to expand the family home for their expanding family. In 1855 they added a second story to their modest cottage, converting it into a much more spacious dwelling worthy of a well-to-do attorney.

Lincoln continued to ride the circuit of county courts for long periods each year (amid a few whispers that he preferred the company of his fellow jurists to that of his occasionally ill-tempered wife and his growing family).

His constant travels through the small towns of Illinois made him a highly recognizable figure, and the friendships he now made would pay political dividends later.

Among the allies Lincoln found in these years was Judge David Davis—as rotund as Lincoln was tall—a transplanted Marylander and Yale Law School graduate who began to play a key role as adviser when Lincoln resumed his political career in the wake of the Kansas-Nebraska Act. Lincoln got himself into a political bind in 1854, when he allowed his name to be place on the ballot for the state legislature. He was elected by a wide margin, but he then declined to serve, angering supporters, in order to pursue a more important position: the U.S. Senate seat from Illinois coming open in 1855. But Lincoln and Davis couldn't corral enough votes in the the year's first legislative session to win it. Lincoln was disappointed, but he was already planning ahead to the 1858 race, when he would run on the new Republican Party ticket, hoping to wrest the other Illinois Senate seat from an ancient enemy, Stephen A. Douglas.

FRANK LESLIE'S ILLUSTRATED

NEWSPAPER

Entered according to Act of Congress, in the year 1857, by FRANK LESLIE, in the Clerk's Office of the District Court for the Southern District of New York. (Copyrighted June 22, 1857.)

No. 82.—VOL. IV.]   **NEW YORK, SATURDAY, JUNE 27, 1857.**   [PRICE 6 CENTS.

TO TOURISTS AND TRAVELLERS.

We shall be happy to receive personal narratives, of land or sea, including adventures and incidents, from every person who pleases to correspond with our paper.

We take this opportunity of returning our thanks to our numerous artistic correspondents throughout the country, for the many sketches we are constantly receiving from them of the news of the day. We trust they will spare no pains to furnish us with drawings of events as they may occur. We would also remind them that it is necessary to send all sketches, if possible, by the earliest conveyance.

VISIT TO DRED SCOTT—HIS FAMILY—INCIDENTS OF HIS LIFE—DECISION OF THE SUPREME COURT.

WHILE standing in the Fair grounds at St. Louis, and engaged in conversation with a prominent citizen of that enterprising city, he suddenly asked us if we would not like to be introduced to Dred Scott. Upon expressing a desire to be thus honored, the gentleman called to an old negro who was standing near by, and our wish was gratified. Dred made a rude obeisance to our recognition, and seemed to enjoy the notice we expended upon him. We found him on examination to be a pure-blooded African, perhaps fifty years of age, with a shrewd, intelligent, good-natured face, of rather light frame, being not more than five feet six inches high. After some general remarks we expressed a wish to get his portrait (we had made

ELIZA AND LIZZIE, CHILDREN OF DRED SCOTT.

efforts before, through correspondents, and failed), and asked him if he would not go to Fitzgibbon's gallery and

have it taken. The gentleman present explained to Dred that it was proper he should have his likeness in the "great illustrated paper of the country," overruled his many objections, which seemed to grow out of a superstitious feeling, and he promised to be at the gallery the next day. This appointment Dred did not keep. Determined not to be foiled, we sought an interview with Mr. Crane, Dred's lawyer, who promptly gave us a letter of introduction, explaining to Dred that it was to his advantage to have his picture taken to be engraved for our paper, and also directions where we could find his domicile. We found the place with difficulty, the streets in Dred's neighborhood being more clearly defined in the plan of the city than on the mother earth; we finally reached a wooden house, however, protected by a balcony that answered the description. Approaching the door, we saw a smart, tidy-looking negress, perhaps thirty years of age, who, with two female assistants, was busy ironing. To our question, "Is this where Dred Scott lives?" we received, rather hesitatingly, the answer, "Yes." Upon our asking if he was home, she said,

"What white man arter dad nigger for?—why don't white man 'tend to his own business, and let dat nigger 'lone? Some of dese days dey'll steal dat nigger—dat are a fact."

DRED SCOTT. PHOTOGRAPHED BY FITZGIBBON, OF ST. LOUIS.

HIS WIFE, HARRIET, PHOTOGRAPHED BY FITZGIBBON, OF ST. LOUIS.

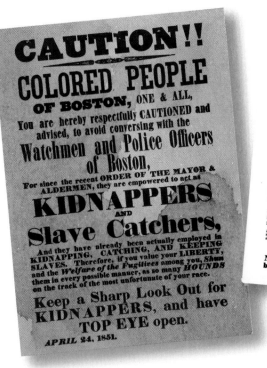

Flash point *Dred Scott's plea for freedom was founded on his residence in Illinois, where slavery had been forbidden by the Northwest Ordinance of 1787 (which predates the U.S. Constitution), and later in the Minnesota Territory, where bondage was forbidden by the Missouri Compromise of 1820.*

In the 1850s the search for slaves seeking refuge in free states brought slavery's horrors into Northern streets. Above left, an 1851 Boston poster urges fugitive slaves to be cautious; at top right, an 1841 poster offers a reward for a runaway slave—in Springfield, Ill. At right is a document granting freedom to a Virginia slave. At left is contemporary national coverage of the Scott case.

Dred Scott, Man without a Country

In 1857 a seemingly unremarkable suit that had been passing through the judicial system for more than a decade was finally decided by the U.S. Supreme Court. But if the case of Dred Scott seemed routine, the court's decision rocked the nation. Scott, a Missouri slave, argued he should be declared free after he spent years with his owners in Illinois and the Minnesota Territory, where slavery was illegal. Chief Justice Roger B. Taney, a Marylander, not only dismissed Scott's claim but also found that even free blacks had no standing to bring a suit in U.S. courts, because they were not citizens—and could never be. In fact, Taney declared, African Americans were "beings of an inferior order, and altogether unfit to associate with the white race, either in social or political relations, and so far inferior that they had no rights which the white man was bound to respect." Or, in short, there was no such thing as an African American.

If the decision's language was shocking, its conclusion was even more far-reaching. Taney and six other Justices determined that, because the U.S. Constitution guarantees property rights and because slaves were a form of property, it was illegal for the Federal Government to prohibit slavery anywhere in the U.S. The Dred Scott decision not only stated that all men were *not* created equal; it also signaled that there could be no more compromises like those of 1820 and 1850—and it set the clock ticking toward almost certain dissolution of the Union. Northerners were appalled, and none more so than Lincoln. The man who had placed his trust in the impartiality of the law could no longer respect the highest U.S. court. The Founders, he argued in 1858, did not mean to say "all were equal in color, size, intellect, moral developments, or social capacity … [but they] did consider all men created equal—equal in 'certain inalienable rights, among which are life, liberty, and the pursuit of happiness.'" By forcing the discussion of slavery back to the founding principles of the nation, Lincoln had begun to embark on the journey that would take him to Gettysburg, where he would ask Americans to reconsecrate themselves to these ideals, in "a new birth of freedom."

With a Single Speech, Lincoln Rouses the Nation

With his bold 1854 address in Peoria attacking the Kansas-Nebraska Act, Lincoln put himself on a trajectory for a direct clash with his old antagonist, Democrat Stephen A. Douglas. Towering above all other anti-slavery voices in Illinois, Lincoln easily won the Republican nomination to oppose Douglas in the Senate election of 1858. On June 16 of that year, he delivered an acceptance speech at the state party convention that soon reached every ear in the nation. His argument was radical—so radical that friends whose advance opinion he sought urged him to reconsider. But Lincoln had long pondered his course, and he was set on it. In the first minutes of the address, he turned, as he often did, to a metaphor from the Bible. Quoting from the Gospels, he diagnosed America as a nation irretrievably riven by slavery and declared, "'A house divided against itself cannot stand.' I believe this government can not endure, permanently, half slave and half free. I do not expect the Union to be dissolved—I do not expect the house to fall—but I do expect it will cease to be divided."

The words were shocking because they gave voice to conclusions many Americans had long believed, but no major politicians had yet dared to express. In today's terms, Lincoln was "out in front of" his audience. He was careful not to anticipate precisely how or when the nation would cease to be divided. But by daring to state what many sensed—that the debilitating debate over slavery was no more than an outworn proxy for the actual confrontation over the practice that had been suppressed since the time of the Founding Fathers—Lincoln seized the national imagination. His speech on division proved unifying: the foes of slavery realized that they at last had found a leader who was prepared to confront slavery's bitter fruits head-on, and come what may.

Breakdown *Americans hurtled ever closer to war in the 1850s. Northerners and Southerners traded insults, demonizing one another in vile terms, and gun-toting Congressmen turned the floor of the U.S. House of Representatives into an armed camp. In May 1856, Senator Charles Sumner of Massachusetts, a fierce Abolitionist, gave a two-day speech in which he attacked many Southern politicians by name, including Senator A.P. Butler of South Carolina. The next day, Preston Brooks, Congressman from South Carolina and Butler's cousin, strode into the Senate chamber and beat Sumner severely with a heavy wooden cane, while friends kept other Senators from intervening. Badly injured, Sumner was unable to return to the Senate until 1859.*

At right is the Illinois Statehouse in Springfield, where Lincoln delivered the "House Divided" speech in 1858.

WHAT LINCOLN SAID

"We are now far into the fifth year, since a policy was initiated, with the avowed object and confident promise, of putting an end to slavery agitation. Under the operation of that policy, that agitation has not only, not ceased, but has constantly augmented. In my opinion, it will not cease, until a crisis shall have been reached, and passed.

"'A house divided against itself cannot stand.' I believe this government cannot endure, permanently half slave and half free. I do not expect the Union to be dissolved—I do not expect the house to fall—but I do expect it will cease to be divided. It will become all one thing or all the other. Either the opponents of slavery will arrest the further spread of it … or its advocates will push it forward, till it shall become alike lawful in all the States, old as well as new—North as well as South."

Showdown in Illinois

Lincoln's magnificent "House Divided" speech thrust him into new prominence as the most eloquent spokesman for the principles of the rapidly growing Republican Party, and there was no question his 1858 race for a U.S. Senate seat from Illinois against his old nemesis, Stephen A. Douglas, would attract national attention. The lives of the two men were strangely intertwined: they first met in 1834 in Vandalia, where Lincoln was a legislator and Douglas a lobbyist. In 1839 the two were admitted to practice before the Illinois Supreme Court on the same day. Both wooed Mary Todd in 1841; both served in the U.S. Congress (Douglas far longer and with more distinction); they opposed each other for the U.S. Senate in 1858 and would do so again for the presidency in 1860.

Yet if their lives matched up, as individuals they were deliciously mismatched: Douglas stood barely over 5 ft. tall and was called "the Little Giant"; Lincoln was an authentic giant. As for their speaking styles, William Herndon sums them up well: the magnetic Douglas was "... full of political history ... eloquent almost to the point of brilliancy, self-confident to the point of arrogance, and a dangerous competitor in every respect." Lincoln's "base was plain common-sense, direct statement, and the inflexibility of logic ... [he] made no effort to dazzle people by his bearing."

The two gifted speakers had shared podiums on several occasions since Lincoln had been lured back into politics by Douglas' controversial Kansas-Nebraska Act. Now, in the 1858 Senate campaign, they agreed to stage a series of seven debates across Illinois. The result was a stirring display of democracy in action, as the two argued over the basic tenets of the U.S. Constitution, the morality of slavery and the legality of its extension into the territories. Huge crowds gathered for the debates, which were staged as back-to-back speeches rather than in a give-and-take format. Lincoln concluded the final debate with a memorable excoriation of slavery: "It is the same spirit that says: 'You work and toil and earn bread, and I eat it.' No matter in what shape it comes, whether from the mouth of a king who seeks to bestride the people of his own nation and live by the fruit of their labor, or from one race of men as an apology for enslaving another race, it is the same tyrannical principle." But despite Lincoln's eloquence, in these days before the direct election of Senators, the Democrats won control of the legislature and Douglas thus became Senator. Once again Lincoln's hopes of securing a national stage for his views were shattered.

"Can the people of a United States Territory, in any lawful way, against the wish of any citizen of the United States, exclude Slavery from its limits prior to the formation of a State Constitution?"

Freeport Question *In the second debate, in Freeport, Ill., Lincoln distilled the argument over popular sovereignty into a single key question, scrawled at left in his hand. Douglas' reply, that the citizens of a territory could indeed restrict slavery prior to writing a state constitution, put him at odds with his Democratic Party's Southern wing, and essentially conceded to Lincoln the argument over slavery's legal extension*

"When [Lincoln] began speaking, his voice was shrill, piping, and unpleasant. His manner, his attitude, his dark, yellow face, wrinkled and dry, his oddity of pose, his diffident movements—everything seemed to be against him, but only for a short time … He never sawed the air nor rent space into tatters and rags as some orators do. He was cool, considerate, reflective … his style was clear, terse, and compact … He was careless of his dress … He despised glitter, show, set forms, and shams." —WILLIAM HERNDON

"My shadow" *On Feb. 27, 1860, the day he delivered the speech at Cooper Union that would lead to his nomination for the presidency, Lincoln had his picture taken by America's best-known photographer, Mathew Brady. The portrait, carefully retouched by Brady to improve Lincoln's appearance, was widely circulated in newspapers. For many Americans, it provided the first glimpse of a politician whose fame was starting to swell. "They have got my shadow," Lincoln said, "and can multiply it indefinitely"*

A Westerner Woos the East

Abraham Lincoln has been placed upon such a lofty pedestal in American life that it's sometimes difficult to picture him as a politician eager for office and working hard to get there. Yet after his loss to Douglas in 1858, Lincoln began to promote himself as a candidate for the presidency. "That man who thinks Lincoln calmly sat down and gathered his robes about him, waiting for the people to call him, has a very erroneous knowledge of Lincoln," law partner William Herndon later wrote. "He was always calculating, and always planning ahead. His ambition was a little engine that knew no rest."

To promote his views more widely, Lincoln oversaw the publication of his debates with Stephen A. Douglas in book form; the volume was issued in the spring of 1860 and soon became a best seller. Aware that he lacked experience on the national stage—he was a four-term state legislator, a one-term U.S. Representative and a two-time loser in races for a U.S. Senate seat—Lincoln knew he must present himself before leading Eastern journalists, businessmen and academics to win the nomination. So he quickly accepted an invitation from the noted Abolitionist clergyman Henry Ward Beecher to address his Brooklyn congregation early in 1860, and he bought a new suit for the occasion.

Enormous public response forced the address to be moved to Cooper Union, below, a new private college in Manhattan, where Lincoln's speech riveted his listeners. Using all his lawyer's tools—rigorous clarity, the careful marshaling of facts and deep research into the original debates that shaped the U.S. Constitution—he constructed a lengthy, three-part address arguing that the Southern position on the extension of slavery into the territories would not have been supported by the Founding Fathers. He concluded with a ringing call for those opposed to slavery to continue the fight: "Let us have faith that right makes might, and in that faith, let us, to the end, dare to do our duty as we understand it."

The Eastern Intelligentsia

Lincoln's swing east early in 1860 was a springboard that launched him to the White House; after the Cooper Union address, he spoke in four New England states. His fame as an orator had grown, thanks to the widely disseminated "House Divided" speech and his debates with Stephen A. Douglas. Eastern power brokers were eager to get a glimpse of this prairie paradox, who was often described as an uncouth, ill-clothed backwoodsman with a fondness for corny jokes yet whose published words rang with eloquence.

Many Eastern Republicans were far more radical in their opposition to slavery than Lincoln was, including the man who invited him to speak in New York. Congregationalist minister Henry Ward Beecher was America's best-known preacher and a devout Abolitionist; he is shown above with his sister, Harriet Beecher Stowe, who had ignited opposition to slavery with her enormous 1852 best seller, *Uncle Tom's Cabin*.

It was the influential Republican newspaper editor Horace Greeley, right, who turned Lincoln's planned remarks at Beecher's Brooklyn church into a political speech in Manhattan. Greeley supported Edward P. Bates for the Republican nomination in 1860 but was a strong Lincoln man in the general election. He generally backed Lincoln's policies as President, though he often found them too moderate.

Convention of 1860

Abraham Lincoln was so far from being considered a prime contender for the Republican presidential nomination in 1860 that his name was seldom mentioned by journalists in the run-up to the gathering. But thanks to savvy supporters, adroit backroom maneuvering, a dash of counterfeiting and some skillful political mythmaking, Lincoln managed to overcome the man widely considered the frontrunner, Senator William H. Seward of New York.

Lincoln and his most trusted political adviser, longtime friend Judge David Davis, concocted a strategy in which they would allow Seward to lead on the first ballot, then would use the Illinois delegation's commitment to Lincoln as a favorite son to accumulate more votes on following ballots. The first challenge was to win the unanimous support of the Illinois delegation, and Lincoln did so in rousing fashion at the state party convention in Decatur the week before the national party met in Chicago. It was at this convention that cheering Lincoln supporters first bore an old pair of fence rails hand-cut by the young Abe into the hall, hailing him as the Rail Splitter. Never mind that Lincoln was currently more a lawyer for railroads than a splitter of rails; the catchy name captured his image as a self-made, incorruptible and humble son of the frontier. Lincoln won the support of the full delegation.

At the convention, whose Chicago site helped energize the Illinois delegates, the strategy worked. No major candidates—New York's Seward, Pennsylvania's Senator Simon Cameron, Ohio's ex-governor Salmon P. Chase and Missouri ex-Congressman Edward Bates—attended the convention, lest they seem too anxious for office. Lincoln, who feared trading favors for promises of support, sent a telegram to Davis: "Make no contracts that will bind me."

On May 18, a crowd of 1,000 Seward men marched behind a brass band to the "Wigwam," the huge, hastily built convention arena, only to find it was full—Lincoln's men had packed it with supporters bearing counterfeit tickets. It was an omen: Seward, as expected, took by far the most votes on the first ballot, 173. It was his high tide, for Davis had persuaded many first-ballot Seward delegates to switch to Lincoln on the second. And they did—including 44 critical voters from Pennsylvania, previously pledged to Cameron. On the second ballot, Seward had 184 votes; Lincoln 181. On the third ballot, Lincoln prevailed. And though he insisted he had made no binding contract to Cameron, Lincoln named him Secretary of War in his Cabinet. Then again, "Honest Abe" also named former rivals Seward, Bates and Chase to his highest council. The Rail Splitter was practiced at the art of mending fences.

"Five thousand people leaped to their seats ... and the wild yell made vesper breathings of all that had preceded. A thousand steam whistles, ten acres of hotel gongs, a tribe of Comanches might have mingled in the scene unnoticed."

—LINCOLN'S FRIEND LEONARD SWETT, ON THE MOMENT WHEN HIS NAME WAS PLACED IN NOMINATION

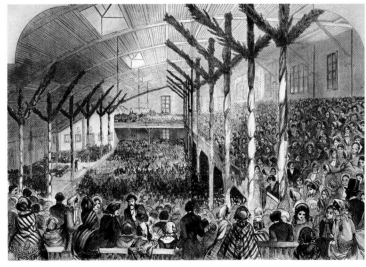

Powwow in Chicago *The Chicago "Wigwam" was completed just before the convention. Although it seated 10,000 people, in a time before amplification, its acoustics were said to be excellent. Lincoln's Illinois supporters controlled the seating, and they put Seward's delegates far away from one another in the hall to make it difficult for them to communicate quickly*

Four-Way Brawl: The 1860 Campaign

Abe Lincoln's supporters cheered him in the 1860 presidential race as the Rail Splitter, a self-made man whose birth in a humble log cabin ensured that his values and views were simple and straightforward. But in fact, Lincoln's character and political views were highly complex—and so was the 1860 presidential campaign. Lincoln and the Republicans faced not one but three opponents, and it is no small irony that the man who diagnosed America's house as irreconcilably divided was thrust into the presidency by that division.

Even before Lincoln was nominated, the fragile Democratic Party, meeting in Charleston, S.C., finally split in two over the issue of slavery. Two Democrats ended up running in the election: Stephen A. Douglas represented the Northern Democrats and incumbent Vice President John C. Breckenridge of Kentucky ran for the Southern Democrats. A further twist was added by the nomination of longtime legislator John Bell of Tennessee by the fledgling Constitutional Union Party, an amalgam of die-hard Whigs and Know-Nothings.

Lincoln did little personal campaigning in the election, as was customary at the time. On Nov. 6, 1860, he followed the course of the voting in Springfield's telegraph office. Lincoln's name was not even on the ballot in many Southern states, so hated was his party, but no matter: Bell and Breckenridge divvied up most of the Southern and border-state votes, and Lincoln won the majority of Northern votes, finally beating his old foe Douglas. Lincoln received 1,866,452 votes, and Douglas 1,376,957. Lincoln carried the Electoral College convincingly, winning 180 votes, as opposed to 72 for Breckenridge, 39 for Bell and 12 for Douglas.

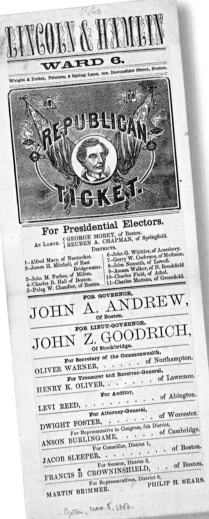

"Abe!" *Election campaigns in the mid-19th century were occasions for those eligible to vote (essentially, white males) to let off steam: it was an era of torchlight processions and bonfires, brass bands and campaign songs, speechifying and catchy slogans ("Tippecanoe and Tyler too!"). Antislavery Republican groups that called themselves "Wide Awake Clubs" rallied support for Lincoln; on the left page is one such group in Mohawk, N.Y., as well as a broadside announcing a Republican rally.*

Above are artifacts from the 1860 campaign. One shortcut, helpful for illiterates, allowed voters to cast ballots by placing a preprinted "ticket" like the one at left in a ballot box. At right is one of the numerous joke books published to showcase Lincoln's brand of frontier humor.

High-Stepping, 1860-Style

This adept political cartoon (artist unknown) depicts the four presidential candidates dancing with their presumed constituents in the wake of the deeply divisive Dred Scott case. In the center, Scott calls the tune. At top left is Southern Democrat John C. Breckenridge, whose partner is incumbent President James Buchanan, head of the party (a.k.a. "Buck," hence the horns). Below them is Northern Democrat Stephen A. Douglas, dancing with a ragged Irish immigrant—a slap at his popularity with despised Catholic voters.

At top right, the antislavery Lincoln, a Republican, dances with a black woman. Below them, the Constitutional Union Party's John Bell partners an Indian brave, a symbol of Know-Nothing nativism.

1861-65
Civil War

At Last, the Crisis

How did the states of the Union become so divided as to make war upon one another? No one has ever improved on the analysis offered by Lincoln in his Second Inaugural Address, delivered only weeks before the South's 1865 surrender: "... four years ago all thoughts were anxiously directed to an impending civil war. All dreaded it, all sought to avert it ... Both parties deprecated war, but one of them would *make* war rather than let the nation survive, and the other would *accept* war rather than let it perish, and the war came.

"One-eighth of the whole population were colored slaves, not distributed generally over the Union, but localized in the southern part of it. These slaves constituted a peculiar and powerful interest. All knew that this interest was somehow the cause of the war. To strengthen, perpetuate, and extend this interest was the object for which the insurgents would rend the Union even by war, while the Government claimed no right to do more than to restrict the territorial enlargement of it."

And the war came. It came with such a headlong rush, triggered by Lincoln's election, that no one was prepared for it: not the North and its slim military; not the South, with a Confederate government just forming; and certainly not the new President, unschooled in war and lacking any Executive experience. "I claim not to have controlled events, but confess plainly that events have controlled me," he would write in 1864. Perhaps, but Lincoln managed to hold a divided North together, find the generals to win the war and begin the essential process of emancipation—before an assassin's bullet killed him in his moment of victory and made him a martyr.

Bird's-eye view *Soldiers observe a Union camp in Cumberland Landing, Va., in 1862*

The Master of the Game

When he arrived in Washington he didn't have much political experience, but Lincoln's emotional strengths made him a natural, argues **Doris Kearns Goodwin**

ABRAHAM LINCOLN'S POLITICAL RESUME WAS MEA-ger, his learning derided and his election considered a stroke of luck. And yet the prairie lawyer from Springfield would emerge the undisputed captain of his distinguished Cabinet, earning the respect of colleagues who had originally disdained him, and become, as Walt Whitman wrote, "the grandest figure yet, on all the crowded canvas of the 19th Century."

As it turned out, unbeknownst to the country at the time, Lincoln was a towering political genius—not because he had mastered the traditional rules of the game but because he possessed a remarkable array of emotional strengths that are rarely found in political life. He had what we would call today a first-class emotional intelligence.

To appreciate the magnitude of Lincoln's political success, it helps to understand just how slight a figure he ap-

peared to be when he arrived in Washington. "Never did a President enter upon office with less means at his command," Harvard professor James Russell Lowell wrote in 1863. "All that was known of him was that he was a good stump-speaker, nominated for his availability—that is, because he had no history." His entire national political experience consisted of a single term in Congress that had come to an end nearly a dozen years earlier and two failed Senate races. He had absolutely no administrative experience and only one year of formal schooling. Newspapers described him as "a third-rate Western lawyer" and a "fourth-rate lecturer, who cannot speak good grammar."

Historian Doris Kearns Goodwin wrote this article in 2005 for a TIME *cover story on Lincoln; her best-selling book on Lincoln's cabinet,* Team of Rivals, *was pubished the same year*

In contrast, his three chief rivals for the Republican nomination were household names in Republican circles. William Henry Seward had been a celebrated Senator from New York for more than a decade and governor of his state for two terms before he went to Washington. Ohio's Salmon P. Chase, too, had been both Senator and governor, and had played a central role in the formation of the Republican Party. Edward Bates was a widely respected elder statesman from Missouri, a former Congressman whose opinions on national matters were still widely sought. All three men, knowing they were better educated, more experienced and more qualified than Lincoln, were stunned when he received the Republican nomination and went on to win the election.

Then he, in turn, stunned the political world by putting all three of his rivals into his Cabinet. It was a seemingly dangerous act, since it risked building up a potential opponent in the next election and ensured that he would be seen by many as a mere figurehead. His opponents were certain that he had failed this first test of leadership. In fact, it was a subtle perception about what he needed, and a deep emotional strength, that lay behind Lincoln's move. As his secretary, John Nicolay, later wrote, Lincoln's "first decision was one of great courage and self-reliance." A less confident man might have surrounded himself with personal supporters who would never question his authority. Later Lincoln was asked why he had chosen his chief rivals for his official family, knowing each of them was still smarting from his loss. Lincoln's answer was simple and shrewd: "We needed the strongest men of the party in the Cabinet. We needed to hold our own people together. I had looked the party over and concluded that these were the very strongest men. Then I had no right to deprive the country of their service."

The decision to appoint his political enemies to his Cabinet was perhaps the most obvious example of his emotional strength. But there were many others, all of which highlighted a different aspect of it.

EMPATHY

Perhaps the most important of his emotional abilities was empathy—the gift of putting himself in the place of others, to experience what they were feeling, to understand their motives and desires. Even as a child, he was uncommonly tenderhearted. He once stopped and tracked back half a mile to rescue a pig caught in a mire—not because he loved the pig, recollected a friend, "just to take a pain out of his own mind." As a young member of the state legislature, he

Frozen *Limited by the technology of the time, photographs of Lincoln, like this 1863 picture, reveal the melancholy strain that was part of his nature. But we have no pictures that capture his celebrated animation, contagious laugh and flashing eyes*

was known for his insight into the opposition's strategy. Even after leaving the body, he would be called upon by his Whig colleagues not only to predict the moves that their Democratic opponents were likely to take but to spell out the countermeasures needed to block them.

Unusual among antislavery orators in the 1850s, Lincoln sought to comprehend the Southerners' position through empathy rather than castigate slave owners as corrupt and un-Christian men. He argued, "They are just what we would be in their situation. If slavery did not now exist amongst them, they would not introduce it. If it did now exist amongst us, we should not instantly give it up." It was useless, he explained in another address, to employ "thundering tones of anathema and denunciation," for denunciation would be met by denunciation, "anathema with anathema."

Far better, he believed, to reach into the heart of one's opponents—which, of course, he memorably did in his second Inaugural when he suggested that the sin of slavery was shared by North and South. "Both read the same Bible, and pray to the same God; and each invokes His aid against the other … let us judge not that we be not judged." In the largest sense, Lincoln's empathy allowed him to absorb the sorrows and hopes of his countrymen, to sense their shifting moods so he could shape and mold their opinion with the right words and the right deeds at the right time.

HUMOR

Though a strain of melancholy was part of his nature, Lincoln possessed a remarkable sense of humor and a gift for storytelling that allowed him, time and again, to defuse tensions and relax his colleagues at difficult moments. Many of his stories, taken from his seemingly limitless stock, were directly applicable to a point being argued. Many were self-deprecatory; all were hilarious. When he began one of them, his "eyes would sparkle with fun," one old-timer remembered, "and when he reached the point in his narrative which invariably evoked the laughter of the crowd, nobody's enjoyment was greater than his."

MAGNANIMITY

He refused to bear grudges or pay people back for previous hurts. While his colleagues tended to let things fester and brooded over perceived slights, he argued that "no man resolved to make the most of himself has time to waste on personal contention." So rare in a politician, this attitude allowed him to form friendships and alliances with those who had previously opposed him. In the 1850s, Edwin Stanton had humiliated him when they were partners in a law case, referring to him as a "long-armed ape," refusing to deal with him as an equal, deliberately shunning him at a hotel, never even opening the brief he had painstakingly prepared.

Yet when the time came for Lincoln to replace Simon Cameron, his first Secretary of War, he appointed Stanton, believing him to be the best man for the all-important post. He recognized that the very qualities that had brought the hotheaded Stanton to treat him badly—his intensity, his bluntness, his determination to succeed—were precisely the qualities he needed in his War Secretary.

GENEROSITY OF SPIRIT

When Congress voted to censure Cameron for wasteful contracts given out to suppliers in the early days of the war, in which middlemen had made off with scandalous profits for unworkable pistols, for blind horses and for knapsacks that disintegrated in the rain, Lincoln publicly took the blame. He explained that the unfortunate contracts were part and parcel of the emergency situation that faced the government in those first days of the war. If fault was to be found, then he himself and his entire Cabinet "were at least equally responsible." For this, Cameron would be forever grateful. Similarly, colleagues of Lincoln were grateful when he shared credit for successes. When General Ulysses S. Grant, the hero of Vicksburg and Chattanooga, arrived in the nation's capital in March 1864 to take command of all the Union armies, he was greeted as a conquering hero at a White House reception. Standing to the side, Lincoln willingly ceded the place of honor he normally occupied, fully aware, as few other ambitious politicians would have been, that "the path to ambition" was wide enough, as an observer phrased it, for the two of them "to walk it abreast."

Above all, he was quick to concede error. When Grant was moving toward Vicksburg, Lincoln thought he "should go down the river," where he could meet up with General Nathaniel Banks. Instead, Grant decided to turn northward. "I feared it was a mistake," Lincoln acknowledged after Grant's spectacular victory. "I now wish to make the personal acknowledgment that you were right, and I was wrong." Then, to lessen the censure of another general, Lincoln wrote, "I frequently make mistakes myself, in the many things I am compelled to do hastily."

PERSPECTIVE

In one characteristic story, a Congressman had received Lincoln's authorization for something to be carried out by the War Department. When War Secretary Stanton refused to honor the order, the disappointed petitioner returned to Lincoln, telling him that Stanton had not only countermanded the order but had called the President a damn fool for issuing it. "Did Stanton say I was a damn fool?" Lincoln asked. "He did, sir, and repeated it." At which point, the President remarked, "If Stanton said I

was a damn fool, then I must be one, for he is nearly always right and generally says what he means. I will step over and see him."

SELF-CONTROL

When angry at someone, Lincoln would occasionally write a hot letter, but then would invariably put it aside until he had cooled down, at which point he no longer needed to send it. Lincoln had rarely been more "dejected and discouraged," as Secretary of the Navy Gideon Welles observed, than when he learned that General George Meade had allowed Robert E. Lee's army to escape after Gettysburg. In a frank letter to Meade, Lincoln acknowledged that he was "distressed immeasureably" by "the magnitude of the misfortune … He was within your easy grasp, and to have closed upon him would, in connection with our other late successes, have ended the war. As it is, the war will be prolonged indefinitely." But Lincoln delayed sending it, knowing the great pain it would cause the general, until his emotions settled down. And when they did, he placed the letter in an envelope on which he wrote, "To Gen. Meade, never sent, or signed." By such gestures, repeated again and again, he repaired injured feelings that might have escalated into lasting animosity.

A SENSE OF BALANCE

In contrast to most of his colleagues who worked themselves to the point of exhaustion, Lincoln understood the importance of finding ways to relax. In the evenings, he regularly entertained friends by reading aloud from Shakespeare, sharing a favorite poem or telling a few of his inexhaustible stories. His ability to think creatively and retain an even keel was rooted in the constructive ways he would dispel worry and anxiety. In the most difficult moments of his presidency, nothing brought him more refreshment and repose than immersing himself in a play. The manager of Grover's Theatre in Washington estimated that Lincoln had come "more than a hundred times" during his presidency. During a performance of *Henry IV*, one of his assistants observed, "He has forgotten the war. He has forgotten Congress. He is out of politics. He is living in Prince Hal's time."

A SOCIAL CONSCIENCE

Lincoln's ambition was never simply for office or power, but rather to accomplish something worthy that would stand the test of time, that would allow his story to be told after he died. His spacious ambition propelled him forward—through his laborious efforts to educate himself, his willingness to try again to reach the state legislature, the death of his first love, Ann Rutledge, and his incapacitating depression during the winter of 1841, when he was in his early 30s. His decision to break off his engagement to Mary Todd had left him devastated, not only because he had hurt Mary but also because he had long considered his ability to keep his word "as the only, or at least the chief, gem of [his] character." Now he could no longer trust himself in that regard.

His biggest political project had fallen apart during this same period. Throughout what eventually turned out to be four terms in the state legislature, he had championed government support for a series of public works to construct bridges, roads and canals so that people in rural areas could bring produce to market. He believed, he later said, that the "leading object" of government was to "lift artificial weights from all shoulders—to clear the path of laudable pursuit for all—to afford all, an unfettered start, and a fair chance, in the race of life." When a depression hit the state in the late 1830s, however, his plans were stopped in midstream. As a major proponent of the costly system that had contributed to his state's travails, Lincoln received a significant share of the blame. Now, beyond sadness over a lost love, he carried the added burden of a damaged reputation and forlorn hopes for the future.

"I am now the most miserable man living," he wrote a friend at the time. "If what I feel were equally distributed to the whole human family, there would not be one cheerful face on the earth. Whether I shall ever be better I can not tell; I awfully forebode I shall not. To remain as I am is impossible; I must die or be better, it appears to me."

His friends were worried that he was suicidal and removed all razors and knives from his room. Throughout the nadir of Lincoln's depression, his best friend, Joshua Speed, stayed by his side. In a conversation both men would remember as long as they lived, Speed warned Lincoln that if he did not rally, he would most certainly die. Lincoln replied that he was more than willing to die, but that he had "done nothing to make any human being remember that he had lived," and that "to link his name with something that would redound to the interest of his fellow man was what he desired to live for."

Even in this moment of despair, the strength of Lincoln's desire to leave "the world a little better for my having lived in it" carried him forward. It became his lodestar, providing a set of principles and standards to guide his everyday actions.

Not long after he signed the Emancipation Proclamation, his old friend Speed visited him at the White House. Lincoln reminded him of their talks during his depression two decades earlier. "I believe that in this measure," Lincoln said, referring to the proclamation, "my fondest hopes will be realized." Nearly two centuries after his birth, we can say with certainty that the ambition that powered Lincoln from his earliest days—the desire to establish an admirable reputation on earth so that his story could be told after he died—has been realized far beyond his fondest hopes. ∎

Abe's Bold Cabinet Choices Keep your friends close—and your enemies closer

WILLIAM SEWARD

AS A RIVAL
Considered a shoo-in for the Republican nomination in 1860, the New York Senator lost to Lincoln on the third ballot.

AS SECRETARY OF STATE
Although they differed on the makeup of the Cabinet and the crucial decision of whether to resupply Fort Sumter as tensions between North and South grew, the pair ended up close friends.

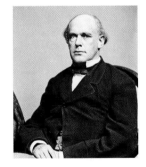

SALMON P. CHASE

AS A RIVAL
The radical Senator from Ohio could muster only 49 votes of 233 needed for the 1860 nomination.

AS TREASURY SECRETARY
Chase, whose job was to finance the war, was frustrated with the conflict's slow pace. He resigned in June 1864 and briefly vied for the nomination. But Lincoln made him U.S. Chief Justice in December 1864.

EDWARD BATES

AS A RIVAL
The conservative Bates hailed from Missouri, a slaveholding border state, which supporters believed made him the ideal candidate in 1860 to avert secession.

AS ATTORNEY GENERAL
Bates railed against Lincoln's loose management style and feuded with other Cabinet members, but he did respect the President. After Lincoln's re-election, he resigned.

EDWIN STANTON

AS A RIVAL
A prominent lawyer who had served as Attorney General under Lincoln's predecessor, Stanton thought Lincoln incompetent.

AS SECRETARY OF WAR
Stanton joined the Cabinet in 1862 after previous Secretary, Simon Cameron, resigned amid scandal. Ruthlessly efficient, Stanton ruffled feathers but, like Seward, grew personally close to Lincoln.

WHAT LINCOLN SAID

"We are not enemies, but friends. We must not be enemies. Though passion may have strained, it must not break our bonds of affection. The mystic chords of memory, stretching from every battlefield and patriot grave to every living heart and hearthstone all over this broad land, will yet swell the chorus of the Union, when again touched, as surely they will be, by the better angels of our nature."

To Preserve, Protect and Defend the Constitution

Abraham Lincoln entered Washington, D.C., to take up his new office in an unfortunately ignominious fashion. After leaving Springfield by train on Feb. 11, his traveling party made a long, winding journey that took him to scores of cities in the North, at each of which he spoke to crowds, assuring them that he would take a firm stand against the Southern states, where secession was already passing from threat to reality. In Westfield, N.Y., he met the 11-year-old girl, Grace Bedell, who had written him a letter after the election encouraging him to grow a beard, and he noted that he had followed her advice. Near the end of the journey, Lincoln was due to pass through Baltimore. But Maryland was a slave state, where Southern sympathies ran deep. Private detective Allan Pinkerton, assigned to protect Lincoln, caught wind of a possible assassination plot. He concocted a ruse in which Lincoln arrived incognito in Baltimore, then secretly changed trains to ensure a safe entrance in Washington. When a journalist reported, incorrectly, that the soft hat Lincoln wore as part of his disguise was a tam-o'-shanter, newspapers gleefully ran cartoons of the lanky Lincoln clad in a Scottish kilt, dancing a Highland fling before sneaking into the capital city.

If Lincoln's arrival in Washington was farcical, the challenge that faced him was tragic. By Inauguration Day, March 4, 1861, seven Southern states had seceded from the Union, and others were close to doing so. Representatives from six states had met in Montgomery, Ala., to form the Confederate States of America, and South Carolina militia troops had fired on a U.S. warship, halting its attempt to bring supplies to Fort Sumter in Charleston Harbor. Abraham Lincoln and the North had a full-scale rebellion on their hands.

In the days before the Inauguration, Lincoln met with the members of his new Cabinet—some of them former rivals for the presidency—consulted with Senators and Representatives and met with General Winfield Scott, the aged veteran of the War of 1812 and Mexican War. "Old Fuss and Feathers" now commanded the U.S. Army, an untested force of only 16,000 men when Lincoln took office.

On Inauguration Day, Lincoln and retiring President James Buchanan rode to the Capitol building in an open carriage (stung in Baltimore, Lincoln overruled security advisers, who asked him to ride in a closed coach). Lincoln's Inaugural Address was a compelling restatement of his political view of the state of the Union. He repeated his belief that the Union was older than the Constitution; dating it to the Continental Congress of 1774, he insisted that it was even older than the Declaration of Independence. He again repeated he would not interfere with slavery in the South and had no legal right to do so. But he also declared he would take all legal measures to oppose what he described as an illegal uprising against the Union rather than a lawful severing of it. In his stirring peroration, adapted and dramatically improved by Lincoln from suggested text provided by William Seward, the new President emphasized that the North and South must not become enemies, for they were united by "the mystic chords of memory."

Unfinished business *The U.S. Capitol was partially covered in scaffolding as work continued on building its dome when Lincoln took the oath of office. He insisted the work continue during the war, as a sign of the endurance of the Union. Above is a* Harper's Weekly *illustration of Lincoln and Buchanan proceeding to the inauguration*

All the President's Men

His lack of military experience didn't stop Lincoln from micromanaging the war. Three years and seven generals later, he found the man to match

From the moment the war started, Abraham Lincoln was surrounded. Across the Potomac was the Confederacy; in Washington was a Cabinet unsure of his abilities, an increasingly hostile Congress and a growing list of Union generals with sensitive egos but alarmingly few victories on the battlefield.

As the war's shocking toll mounted, Lincoln turned from commander to commander,

looking for the man who would protect Washington from rebel armies and press the Union's biggest advantage: "We have the greater numbers."

Lincoln had no real military experience except for 77 combat-free days in an Illinois militia, but he became an avid strategist, continually peppering field leaders with questions, suggestions, precise orders and emphatic, if often ignored, exhortations

to drive against the enemy.

By 1864 he had found his fighter. When Ulysses S. Grant took command in the East, Lincoln didn't, for once, demand specific plans. Six weeks later Grant had lost more men than every general before him, but Robert E. Lee's army was bottled up in Petersburg, Va. "Hold on with a bull-dog grip," Lincoln urged Grant. Unlike his predecessors, Grant did.

GENERAL DISAPPOINTMENT
Lincoln professed to Grant that he just wanted someone to "take the responsibility and act." But as Robert E. Lee's legend grew, so did the list of failed Union commanders

3 POPE[**]
to SECOND BULL RUN
Aug. 28-30, 1862

14,449 | 9,420

WINFIELD SCOTT	1 IRVIN McDOWELL	2, 4 GEORGE McCLELLAN	3 JOHN POPE
Promise "Old Fuss and Feathers" was a national hero from the Mexican War of 1846. He devised the "Anaconda Plan" to blockade the South's ports	**Promise** The fastidious Ohioan didn't drink or smoke. He wanted more time to train the Army, but Lincoln ordered him ahead, saying "They are green also"	**Promise** Undeniably a great organizer, he built the Army of the Potomac and filled it with confidence. He then hatched a plan to capture Richmond from the south	**Promise** A politically connected, boastful man who liked to headline his dispatches "Headquarters in the Saddle." Lee called him a "miscreant"
Peril He nominally commanded the Union armies, but was too old, obese and infirm to lead troops. History would vindicate his strategy	**Peril** His plan for the first big battle at Bull Run was sound, but his Army and his logistics weren't. Union soldiers called their retreat "the Great Skedaddle"	**Peril** An organizer but not a fighter. Sidelined after his Peninsula debacle, he got a second chance at Antietam. He fought to a draw there despite knowing Lee's plans	**Peril** He vowed to "bag the whole lot" of Lee's army on the site of the war's first battle. He didn't, and was banished to Minnesota for the rest of the war. McClellan was back

Map labels:
GETTYS[
TANEYTOW[
ANTIETAM
FREDE[
HARPERS FERRY
LEESBURG
VIRGINIA
BULL RUN
MANASSAS
Grant takes over
DUMFRIES
CULPEPER
AQUIA
CHANCELLORSVILLE
FREDE[BURG
WILDERNESS
SPOTSYLVANIA
LOUISA
MILFORD
ANDERSON
NORTH ANNA
HANOVER COURT HOUSE
COLD HARBOR
RICHMOND
SEVEN PINES
MALVERN HILL
PETERS[

To Appomat[
Lee surren[
April 9, 186[

*Killed, woun[captured and missing

**Pope's com[was called th[of Virginia

Note: Map boundaries a[1863, when V[Virginia beca[separate stat[

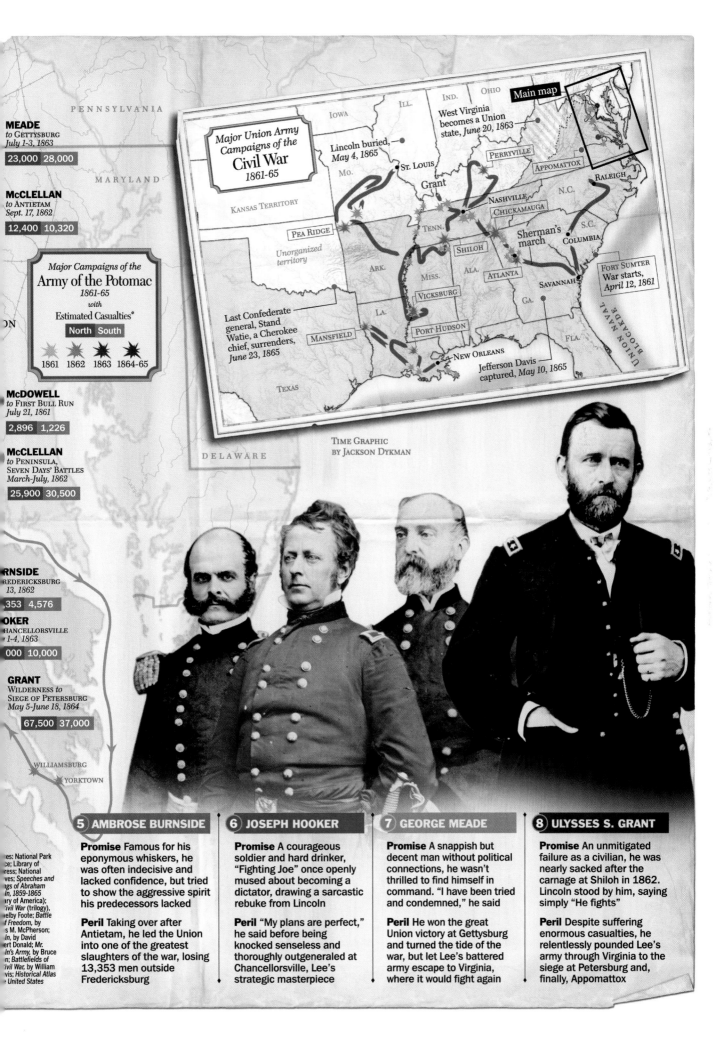

MEADE
to GETTYSBURG
July 1-3, 1863

23,000 28,000

McCLELLAN
to ANTIETAM
Sept. 17, 1862

12,400 10,320

Major Campaigns of the
Army of the Potomac
1861-65
with
Estimated Casualties*

North South

1861 1862 1863 1864-65

McDOWELL
to FIRST BULL RUN
July 21, 1861

2,896 1,226

McCLELLAN
to PENINSULA,
SEVEN DAYS' BATTLES
March-July, 1862

25,900 30,500

RNSIDE
REDERICKSBURG
13, 1862

353 4,576

OKER
HANCELLORSVILLE
1-4, 1863

000 10,000

GRANT
WILDERNESS to
SIEGE OF PETERSBURG
May 5-June 18, 1864

67,500 37,000

WILLIAMSBURG
YORKTOWN

PENNSYLVANIA
MARYLAND
DELAWARE

*Major Union Army
Campaigns of the*
Civil War
1861-65

IOWA ILL. IND. OHIO
West Virginia
becomes a Union
state, June 20, 1863

Main map

Lincoln buried,
May 4, 1865
St. Louis
Mo.
Grant
PERRYVILLE
APPOMATTOX
RALEIGH

KANSAS TERRITORY
NASHVILLE
CHICKAMAUGA
N.C.

PEA RIDGE
TENN.
SHILOH
Sherman's
march
COLUMBIA
S.C.

Unorganized
territory
ARK.
MISS. ALA.
ATLANTA
SAVANNAH
FORT SUMTER
War starts,
April 12, 1861

VICKSBURG
GA.

Last Confederate
general, Stand
Watie, a Cherokee
chief, surrenders,
June 23, 1865
MANSFIELD
LA.
PORT HUDSON
FLA.

UNION NAVAL BLOCKADE

TEXAS
NEW ORLEANS
Jefferson Davis
captured, May 10, 1865

TIME GRAPHIC
BY JACKSON DYKMAN

es: National Park
ce; Library of
ress; National
ves; Speeches and
ngs of Abraham
n, 1859-1865
ary of America);
ivil War (trilogy),
elby Foote; Battle
f Freedom, by
s M. McPherson,
n, by David
ert Donald; Mr.
n's Army, by Bruce
n; Battlefields of
ivil War, by William
vis; Historical Atlas
United States

---

⑤ AMBROSE BURNSIDE

Promise Famous for his eponymous whiskers, he was often indecisive and lacked confidence, but tried to show the aggressive spirit his predecessors lacked

Peril Taking over after Antietam, he led the Union into one of the greatest slaughters of the war, losing 13,353 men outside Fredericksburg

---

⑥ JOSEPH HOOKER

Promise A courageous soldier and hard drinker, "Fighting Joe" once openly mused about becoming a dictator, drawing a sarcastic rebuke from Lincoln

Peril "My plans are perfect," he said before being knocked senseless and thoroughly outgeneraled at Chancellorsville, Lee's strategic masterpiece

---

⑦ GEORGE MEADE

Promise A snappish but decent man without political connections, he wasn't thrilled to find himself in command. "I have been tried and condemned," he said

Peril He won the great Union victory at Gettysburg and turned the tide of the war, but let Lee's battered army escape to Virginia, where it would fight again

---

⑧ ULYSSES S. GRANT

Promise An unmitigated failure as a civilian, he was nearly sacked after the carnage at Shiloh in 1862. Lincoln stood by him, saying simply "He fights"

Peril Despite suffering enormous casualties, he relentlessly pounded Lee's army through Virginia to the siege at Petersburg and, finally, Appomattox

In South Carolina, War's First Salvos

In the spring of 1861 neither the Union nor the emerging Confederacy was prepared for war, but the rush toward conflict that had begun with Lincoln's election continued to gain steam. By the time he took office, many federal facilities in the seceding states had already been abandoned. The day after his inauguration, Lincoln received word that the group of federal fortifications in the harbor at Charleston, S.C., still fully manned but blockaded by rebel militia and ships, must soon surrender or face starvation. Army chief General Winfield Scott told Lincoln that the federal military lacked the men and equipment to resupply them and that mounting such an expedition would take months of preparation. Defying Scott and others who counseled caution, Lincoln ordered a fleet of Union ships to set sail for Charleston on April 6. He appears to have been resigned to the coming of war and was determined to make the South fire the first shots.

Union commander Major Robert Anderson had secretly evacuated his 127 men to the most defensible of the harbor fortifications, half-built Fort Sumter, in the last week of 1860. After he refused a Confederate call to surrender, South Carolina artillery opened fire on both the fort and the Union fleet in the predawn hours of April 12. The antagonists fired some 4,000 shells in the next 30 hours (above, the damaged fort after the bombardment), as the Union supply ships were repulsed and Anderson's garrison almost ran out of ammunition. The Union commander surrendered Fort Sumter on the following day—but not before using his final shells, with the permission of the victors, to fire a 100-gun salute to the Star-Spangled Banner that no longer united the states. The war had begun.

Bull Run Ushers in a Long, Devastating Conflict

After Fort Sumter, both North and South began preparing for war in earnest, drafting large numbers of troops and purchasing weapons. Leaders on both sides hoped a single decisive battle would end the conflict. Aiming to decapitate the Confederacy, Lincoln's advisers planned a thrust toward the capital of Richmond, Va., only 96 miles from Washington. The first step: to take control of the strategic railroad junction at Manassas, near Bull Run Creek, 30 miles from the District of Columbia. Drawn by what was billed as a historic—even romantic—spectacle, thousands of sightseers, many with children and picnic baskets in tow, accompanied Union General Irvin McDowell's 35,000 troops as they marched toward Virginia in July 1861. Waiting for them were 22,000 Confederate troops commanded by General Pierre G.T. Beauregard.

The soldiers on both sides were novices, and so were their generals. When these amateur armies met on July 21, the battle at first seemed to go at the Union's way, until retreating Confederates were rallied by General Thomas Jackson, soon dubbed "Stonewall" for his firm stand on this day. After 10,000 fresh rebel troops from the Shenandoah Valley arrived at the Manassas rail station, Union troops retreated in disarray. For days afterward, wounded, exhausted and panicked soldiers trickled into Washington, now itself in danger of a Confederate thrust that might bring a Southern victory. But that gambit never came. As General Joseph Johnston, commander of the reinforcements at Bull Run, later wrote, "The Confederate Army was more disorganized by victory than that of the United States by defeat." Above, an 1862 photograph shows several of the hastily dug graves in which some of the deceased soldiers were given field burials.

"*I have just read your dispatch about sore-tongued and fatigued horses. Will you pardon me for asking what the horses of your army have done since the battle at Antietam that fatigues* anything?"

—TELEGRAM FROM THE PRESIDENT TO GENERAL MCCLELLAN, OCT. 25, 1862

More Slaughter, More Stalemate

By the fall of 1862, a string of victories in the Shenandoah Valley and in a bloody sequel to Bull Run had handed momentum to the South and deflated Union morale. An increasingly frustrated Abraham Lincoln struggled to get the vainglorious commander of the Army of the Potomac, General George McClellan, to commit to battle. McClellan, a Democrat with a low opinion of Lincoln and a high opinion of himself, was superb at training his troops but always managed to find reasons to avoid taking the fight to the enemy. His counterpart in the Army of Northern Virginia, General Robert E. Lee, was made of sterner stuff. Sensing the time was right to invade Northern territory, he thrust into Maryland in September. His goal: to put Washington again in danger and force Lincoln to the negotiating table.

As his troops moved to engage Lee, McClellan enjoyed a fantastic stroke of luck: Union soldiers stumbled upon a written copy of Lee's full battle plan. Here was the chance McClellan had been waiting for. "If I cannot whip Bobbie Lee, I will be willing to go home," he told his staff. A massive engagement began on the morning of Sept. 17, near the town of Sharpsburg, alongside Antietam Creek, where the two sides battled to a stalemate in a blizzard of blood. By day's end, almost 25,000 men on both sides were dead, missing or seriously injured. It was slaughter on a scale the North could afford and the South could not. In a single day, the balance had shifted. Now it was the Confederacy that lay open to Union invasion, as Lee's tattered army retreated. For a moment, war's end seemed within Union reach: a single, bold follow-up stroke by McClellan might have destroyed the remnants of Lee's army. But McClellan, true to type, refused to pursue Lee vigorously. Appalled at such timidity, Lincoln visited the battlefield days later and faced down McClellan; two months later, he removed him from command. But the victory, if costly, gave Lincoln an opportunity he had been waiting for: to strike a blow, even if a largely symbolic one, at the South's power to make war, by shutting down its supply of free labor.

Showdown *At left, an angry Lincoln confers with his reluctant top warrior, General George McClellan, at Antietam, after what remains the single bloodiest day of battle in U.S. history. Here Lincoln accused McClellan of being "overcautious."*

Below, Union physician Anson Hurd of the 14th Indiana Infantry Regiment aids wounded rebels after the battle.

Unshackling the Slaves

During his national political career, Abraham Lincoln hewed to a moderate stance among those who hated slavery. Though he firmly opposed its extension into new territories, he did not belong to the Abolitionist wing of his party, and he pledged in his first Inaugural Address he would not interfere with slavery in the South. In his Aug. 2, 1862, response to newspaper editor Horace Greeley on the subject, he stated, "My paramount object in this struggle *is* to save the Union, and is *not* either to save or to destroy slavery. If I could save the Union without freeing *any* slave I would do it, and if could save it by freeing *all* the slaves I would do it; and if I could save it by freeing some and leaving others alone I would also do that."

In this letter Lincoln was carefully establishing his priorities and building a case for setting free the slaves as essential to a military victory that would serve his primary cause of preserving the Union. For even as he wrote to Greeley, he was preparing to emancipate the slaves in the rebel states by presidential decree. This course was compelling on both moral and military grounds: liberating these essential workers, Lincoln knew, would directly attack the economic gears that kept the Confederate war machine working.

Lincoln began to consider issuing an Emancipation Proclamation in the summer of 1862. He convened members of his Cabinet on July 22 to read them a first draft of the document, which he proposed to issue in his role as Commander in Chief of the U.S. military, and which thus reads more as a military document than as a ringing declaration of human rights—and which did not free slaves in the five border states that had not seceded. Secretary of State William Seward argued that the document must not be issued until the Union won a victory in the war or it might be construed as a last-chance gamble of a losing side. Lincoln agreed: he waited until five days after the Union victory in the Battle of Antietam to issue the document.

In the short run, the decree had the expected effect: Abolitionists and most Republicans were thrilled and African Americans rejoiced, while Northern Democrats were outraged. Britons, who had come close to supporting their cotton suppliers in the South, cheered. Many Northern soldiers, however, were horrified; they argued they had enlisted to save the Union rather than to free the slaves. In the long run, Lincoln came to regard emancipation as one of his greatest achievements. After the war's end, the final act of abolition was achieved as Lincoln had long argued it should be: the 13th Amendment to the Constitution, ratified on Dec. 18, 1865, states, "Neither slavery nor involuntary servitude ... shall exist within the United States."

Free at last!
Above, scores of newly freed slaves prepare to depart a cotton plantation near Beaufort, S.C., in 1862.
At right, a detail of black U.S. Army soldiers stands guard in front of a former slave-trading firm in Alexandria, Va., in 1862. A few such groups were accepted into the Army before emancipation, which went into effect on Jan. 1, 1863. It was only after that date that blacks were actively enlisted to serve in segregated units within Union ranks.

The Great Emancipator

Of all the iconic roles assigned to Lincoln in life and death, none has undergone more transformation than his image as the Great Emancipator. It is a part he refused to play in life: when he visited a fallen Richmond, Va., in 1865 and blacks knelt at his feet to thank him, he was appalled and made them desist. But the image was firmly fixed after assassination made him a martyr.

For some 100 years, many African Americans regarded Lincoln as a sort of paternalistic redeemer figure, as depicted in the Currier & Ives lithograph at left, until historians in the 1960s began publicizing the truth: Lincoln shared many of the widespread racist views of his time, long advocated the return of freed blacks to Africa and clearly stated that his primary goal in the Civil War was to preserve the Union rather than free the slaves. These revelations were sometimes used to portray Lincoln as complicit in creating a false mythology.

Today a more nuanced view prevails: as Lincoln's successor Barack Obama wrote in a 2005 essay in TIME: "I cannot swallow whole the view of Lincoln as the Great Emancipator." But he goes on to hail Lincoln's "moral compass" and his courage in tackling the scourge of slavery head-on rather than passing it on to others, as so many had done before him. In short, we no longer need to hail Lincoln as the Great Emancipator to recognize his greatness.

TOP: BETTMANN CORBIS; BOTTOM: WILLIAM R. PYWELL, 1862. LIBRARY OF CONGRESS PRINTS AND PHOTOGRAPHS DIVISION

Across the Great Divide

The friendship between Lincoln and Frederick Douglass required from both a change of heart, notes **John Stauffer**

THE TWO GIANTS COULD HAVE IGNORED EACH OTHER or become enemies. So how is it that Abraham Lincoln and Frederick Douglass, the most famous black man of the 19th century, became friends? And what difference did their friendship make? The answer is that Lincoln recognized early on that he needed the ex-slave to help him destroy the Confederacy and preserve the Union. And so at a time when most whites would not let a black man cross their threshold, the President met Douglass three times at the White House. As for Douglass, at one point he believed that Lincoln was a racist who argued that blacks and whites should be kept apart, but he came to realize that Lincoln's shrewd sense of timing and public opinion would help set free the nation's blacks.

Despite the immense racial gulf separating them, Lincoln and Douglass had a lot in common. They were the two pre-eminent self-made men of their era. Lincoln was born dirt poor, had less than a year of formal schooling and became one of the nation's greatest Presidents. Dou-

glass spent the first 20 years of his life as a slave, had no formal schooling—in fact, his masters forbade him to read or write—and became one of the nation's greatest writers and activists. Though nine years younger, Douglass overshadowed Lincoln as a public figure in the 15 years before the Civil War. He published two best-selling autobiographies before the age of 40, edited his own newspaper beginning in 1847 and was a brilliant orator, even better than Lincoln, at a time when public speaking was a major source of entertainment and power.

The two men shared a love of music and literature and educated themselves (Douglass on the sly while a slave) by reading the same books: Aesop's *Fables*, the Bible, Shakespeare and especially *The Columbian Orator*, a popular anthology of speeches for boys. They were athletic, strong and tall: Douglass was about 6 ft.,

---

John Stauffer is a professor of history and American literature at Harvard. His Giants: The Parallel Lives of Frederick Douglass and Abraham Lincoln *was published in November 2008*

Lincoln 6 ft. 4 in., when the average height for men was 5 ft. 7 in. They were ambitious men and had great faith in the moral and technological progress of their nation. And they both called slavery a sin.

When the Civil War broke out in April 1861, however, they had very different strategies for winning it. Douglass repeatedly urged Lincoln to free the slaves and recruit black soldiers. But Lincoln's aim was to preserve the Union. He feared that if he freed the slaves and ordered black soldiers to kill whites, he would alienate Northern conservatives and lose the border slave states of Delaware, Maryland, Kentucky and Missouri. When Lincoln refused to tap into this source of power, Douglass became frustrated with him. His frustration turned to contempt in August 1862, after Lincoln met with a delegation of African Americans and urged them to immigrate to Central America. "You and we are different races," Lincoln told his black audience. "Even when you cease to be slaves, you are yet far removed from being placed on an equality with the white race." He concluded, "It is better for us both, therefore, to be separated."

Douglass was outraged when Lincoln's words reached him: in Central and South America, he noted, "distinct races live peaceably together in the enjoyment of equal rights" without civil wars. What Douglass did not know was that Lincoln had already drafted a preliminary Emancipation Proclamation but had not made it public. And its final version called for the enlistment of black troops.

With emancipation, Douglass's attitude toward Lincoln suddenly and dramatically changed. Never again would he so harshly criticize the President, even though they continued to disagree on many things. In August 1863, Douglass met with the President for the first time. Since January he had been eagerly recruiting blacks, urging "Men of Color, To Arms!" But black soldiers were being discriminated against. They received about half the pay whites did and were not being promoted for distinguished service.

Douglass went to Washington to plead their case to the President. When he entered the White House, the stairway was filled with petitioners, all of them white men. He thought he would have to wait all day, but within two minutes of sending up his card, a messenger called for him. As he elbowed his way up the stairs, he heard someone remark, "Yes, damn it, I knew they would let the n_____ through." When Lincoln saw Douglass, he rose to greet him. "Mr. Douglass, I know you; I have read about you … Sit down, I am glad to see you." After hearing Douglass's complaints, Lincoln assured him that black soldiers would eventually receive the same pay as white soldiers, and he promised to sign any promotion for blacks the Secretary of War recommended.

Douglass came away from the meeting deeply moved.

What most impressed him was Lincoln's honesty and sincerity—"There was no vain pomp and ceremony about him … In his company I was never in any way reminded of my humble origin, or of my unpopular color." He sensed a kindred spirit in Lincoln, someone "whom I could love, honor, and trust without reserve or doubt." The respect was mutual; Lincoln regarded Douglass as "one of the most meritorious men, if not the most meritorious man, in the United States."

A year later, in August 1864, Lincoln decided that he needed Douglass and requested a second, urgent meeting with him. He wanted Douglass to organize a band of black scouts "to go into the rebel states, beyond the lines of our armies, and carry the news of emancipation, and urge the slaves to come within our boundaries," as Douglass recalled. If the plan worked, it would preserve the Union and end slavery. An amazed Douglass eagerly accepted Lincoln's proposal and began preparing for the invasion. Sherman's victory at Atlanta, however, rendered the plan unnecessary.

WHAT LINCOLN SAID

> *"If slavery is not wrong, nothing is wrong. I can not remember when I did not so think, and feel."*

When Douglass and Lincoln met for the third time, in March 1865, the mood was celebratory and they considered each other friends. Douglass came to Washington to attend Lincoln's second Inauguration. The war was almost over; some 179,000 blacks were in uniform, marching in triumph through the South; and the new 13th Amendment abolished slavery throughout the U.S.

Douglass thought Lincoln's address sounded "more like a sermon than a state paper." After the ceremony he went to the reception at the White House—where two policemen rudely yanked him aside and told him no persons of color were allowed to enter. Douglass said no such order could have come from the President. The police refused to yield, until Douglass sent word to Lincoln and he was admitted. Douglass found him in the elegant East Room, standing "like a mountain pine in his grand simplicity and homely beauty."

"Here comes my friend," Lincoln said, taking Douglass by the hand. "I am glad to see you. I saw you in the crowd today, listening to my Inaugural Address." He asked Douglass how he liked it, adding, "There is no man in the country whose opinion I value more than yours." "Mr. Lincoln," Douglass replied, "that was a sacred effort." ■

Another Defeat for Lincoln's Army

The hard-won Union victory at Antietam in the early fall of 1862 offered President Lincoln the chance to launch two major initiatives: he issued the Emancipation Proclamation, and in November 1862, he finally removed the popular but ineffectual General George McClellan from command of the Army of the Potomac. Lincoln and his new top military adviser, General Henry W. Halleck, named General Ambrose Burnside to replace McClellan. Earlier in 1862, Burnside had led a Union amphibious assault that shut down a key Southern port in North Carolina.

Halleck described the Army of the Potomac under McClellan as "an inert mass." Yet Burnside soon proved just as incapable as "Little Mac" of instilling it with the vigor and discipline needed to make it an offensive force. When Lincoln and Halleck directed him to launch an attack against the Confederate capital of Richmond, Va., the effort was plagued by familiar problems of hesitancy and poor organization. Designed to strike with surprise and dispatch, the campaign was carried out so slowly that Southern troops under General Robert E. Lee were well dug in by the time Burnside ordered Union soldiers to attack them outside Fredericksburg, Va., on Dec. 13, 1862. The result was an exercise in slaughter, as no fewer than 14 brigades of Northern troops crossed an open field in an uphill attack under withering Southern fire. By day's end, some 13,000 Union troops were dead or wounded, while the South suffered only 5,000 casualties.

The colossal defeat left Lincoln in one of the weakest positions of his presidency. A chorus of Northern voices denounced him, and Republican Senators schemed to replace his entire Cabinet, though Lincoln thwarted them. "If there is a worse place than hell, I am in it," Lincoln said, apparently so depressed that he came close to despair. "We are now on the brink of destruction. It appears to me that the Almighty is against us."

Prelude to battle *Soldiers of the 1st New Jersey Infantry Division hunker down in trenches as Union officers survey the landscape around Fredericksburg. The black soldier at right may have been among the first African Americans to serve in Union ranks, which were first opened to black recruits after Lincoln issued the Emancipation Proclamation earlier in 1862*

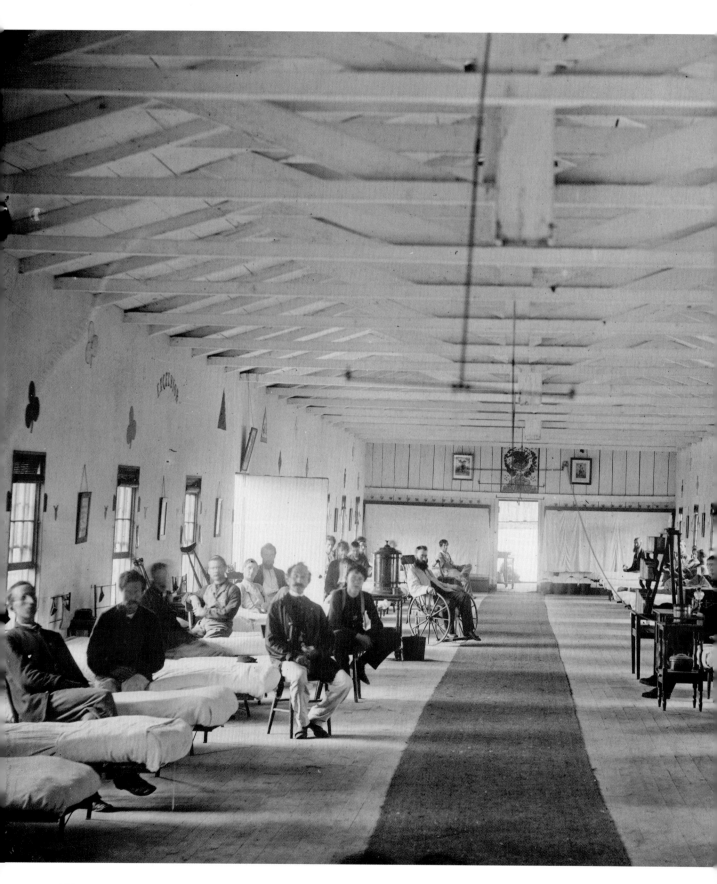

Terrible Swift Sword

The Civil War caused more casualties than all the other conflicts in U.S. history through 2008—combined. According to the U.S. Department of Veterans Affairs, some 250,000 of the 3 million men who served died in combat: roughly 140,000 Union soldiers and 75,000 Confederates. Nearly 300,000 more died off the battlefield, almost always by disease, while another quarter-million were seriously wounded. And that's only the military toll, which excludes the untold tens of thousands of civilians who were maimed, starved or killed amid the war's carnage and chaos. In the 1860s, there was no way of tracking such figures. The subject is throughly explored by historian and Harvard University president Drew Gilpin Faust in *This Republic of Suffering: Death and the American Civil War* (Knopf; 2008).

Part of the war's cost was imposed by the primitive state of 19th century medicine. Lacking antibiotics or anesthetics, military surgeons could often do little more than keep wounded soldiers warm. With scant knowledge of proper sanitary procedures, doctors may have hurt more soldiers than they helped: million of cases of typhus, dysentery and gangrene were reported. When surgeons did intervene, it was often to amputate an arm or a leg—a procedure that generally involved a hacksaw and a bullet to clamp one's teeth on and took about 90 seconds. Union Army surgeon William Keen, who began treating wounded soldiers after just four months in medical school, later wrote, "We operated in old, bloodstained and often pus-stained coats … with clean hands in the social sense, but they were undis-infected hands."

Yet if the science of saving lives was still primitive, the technology used to end them was making great strides, as new killing machines made Civil War battlefields efficient factories of death. The Gatling gun, an early type of machine gun first used in battle in 1861, could fire 1,000 rounds per minute, while new rifles with grooved barrels offered improved range and accuracy.

The terrible cost of the conflict haunted the melancholy Lincoln, who gave up hunting at age 7 after he regretted killing a turkey. He once said to a Congressman: "Doesn't it strike you as queer that I, who couldn't cut the head off of a chicken, and who was sick at the sight of blood, should be cast into the middle of a great war, with blood flowing all about me?" His fatalistic turn of mind led him to wonder, as he did in his Second Inaugural Address, if the war was divine retribution for the sins of slavery, and that "every drop of blood drawn with the lash shall be paid by another drawn with the sword."

Recuperating *Wounded soldiers recover at the Union Army's Armory Square Hospital in Washington—a quiet, staid contrast to the makeshift combat hospitals on the front, where doctors struggled to keep wounded soldiers alive using primitive medical techniques amid the chaos of battle. The 1,000-bed building was located on the National Mall, where the Smithsonian Institution's National Air and Space Museum stands today; it was demolished in 1964*

The Union Turns the Tide: Vicksburg

Two battles decided in the first week of July 1863—one a strategic masterstroke and the other an accident—all but sealed the defeat of the Confederacy. One Union victory came on the western front, at Vicksburg, Miss., on the Mississippi River. After the fall of New Orleans in May 1862, Southern control of the vital waterway hinged on this "Gibraltar of the Confederacy," located on bluffs overlooking a bend in the river. Hard-driving Union General Ulysses S. Grant surrounded this natural fortress and lay siege to it in the spring of 1863.

Within weeks, the 35,000 people inside Vicksburg, civilians and soldiers alike, were starving. Reduced to eating rats, residents moved into caves to avoid the relentless fire of more than 200 Union artillery pieces. At last, on July 4, Vicksburg surrendered. In a single stroke, control of the Mississippi, of the last remaining rail link across it and of all the rich resources on its western side, were taken from the Confederacy. The South was effectively split in two, and some 30,000 Confederate soldiers were taken prisoner. Grant released them and sent them home, rather than expending resources on transporting and caring for them. Lincoln had once said, "Vicksburg is the key! The war can never be brought to a close until that key is in our pocket." Now he rejoiced that "the Father of Waters again goes unvexed to the sea."

The Union Turns the Tide: Gettysburg

A momentous victory closer to home also brightened Lincoln's spirits. Mounting his last invasion of the North, Robert E. Lee had stabbed into Pennsylvania in May. As rebel troops probed toward Harrisburg, neither side expected a battle at the town where they stumbled onto each other's path on July 1: Gettysburg. But stubborn Union defenses in the area caused Lee to concentrate his forces in the town, drawing Union reinforcements. Deprived of his two most trusted lieutenants, Thomas ("Stonewall") Jackson (killed in May) and cavalry officer J.E.B. Stuart (who arrived late), Lee made a rare and disastrous tactical error. On July 2 he ordered General George Pickett to send successive waves of men, more than 15,000 in all, charging across an open field toward the Union artillery line. They were cut down by the thousands.

Battered and bloodied, Lee's army began retreating to Virginia the next day. At the end of the war's largest engagement, more than 50,000 soldiers on both sides were killed, wounded, captured or missing. Now, yet another Union general, George Meade, refused pursuit and allowed Lee to fight another day. Lincoln, again furious at opportunity lost, began to imagine how things might be different if the gritty victor at Vicksburg, Grant, were put in command of all Union forces.

Turning points
Opposite, Union troops bombard the fortress city of Vicksburg. Above, slain rebels are placed in rows in a field at Gettysburg

103

They Said He Was A Lousy Speaker

His style could be too plain for the taste of his time, but
Douglas L. Wilson explains why Lincoln speaks powerfully to us

N O AMERICAN WRITER'S WORDS ARE MORE ADMIRED than those of Abraham Lincoln. By the time of his assassination in 1865, he had written passages by which everything that followed would be measured. But such an ability was the last thing the American public expected from the obscure prairie lawyer who took office just four years earlier. "We have a President without brains," wrote the country's leading historian, George Bancroft. Bancroft was, admittedly, a Democrat, but many self-respecting Republicans were also concerned about the implications of having an untried, self-educated "rail splitter" as a leader in a time of grave national crisis. Charles Francis Adams, a leading Republican and the son and grandson of Presidents, wrote of the new President-elect in his diary: "Good natured, kindly, honest, but frivolous and uncertain." The doubts and fears of many Americans were expressed by a newspaper editor who asked, "Who will write this ignorant man's state papers?"

The Northern intelligentsia was initially blind to Lin-

coln's writing ability for at least two reasons. First, there was the strong impression, reinforced by his unkempt appearance and awkward demeanor, that he was a rube. His obvious discomfort in formal clothes on ceremonial occasions and his constant fidgeting with his ill-fitting kid gloves did little to dispel those misgivings. Moreover, he insisted on entertaining sophisticated visitors by telling country stories in a broad hoosier accent. Wall Street lawyer George Templeton Strong wrote in his diary after their first meeting that the President was a "barbarian," a "yahoo." And Strong liked him.

Another reason Lincoln's writing ability was underrated was that his typically plain diction and straightforward expression were at odds with the public's expectations. The recognized standard for a statesmanlike address in mid-19th century America called for consider-

Douglas L. Wilson is a co-director of the Lincoln Studies Center at Knox College in Galesburg, Ill.

ably more formality and pretension. The prose of acknowledged masters of that kind of writing—such as Lincoln's fellow orator at Gettysburg, Edward Everett, or Massachusetts Senator Charles Sumner—generally featured elevated diction, self-consciously artful expression and a certain moral unction. Lincoln's insistence on direct and forthright language, by contrast, seemed "odd" or "peculiar," as in this passage from a public letter he sent to Horace Greeley, founder and editor of the New York *Tribune*, an antislavery paper: "My paramount object in this struggle is to save the Union, and is not either to save or to destroy slavery. If I could save the Union without freeing any slave I would do it, and if I could save it by freeing all the slaves I would do it; and if I could save it by freeing some and leaving others alone I would also do that."

When discerning observers noticed that his words had power, they often assumed that someone else must have written them. His Secretary of State, William H. Seward, was a noted orator and wordsmith who was thought to have had a hand in Lincoln's first Inaugural. That was in fact true, but few of Seward's suggested changes were stylistic improvements, and we know from the manuscript that his chief contribution—a more conciliatory ending—was brilliantly rewritten by Lincoln. The Secretary of the Treasury, Salmon P. Chase, was sometimes thought to be responsible for Lincoln's best work, and occasionally it was credited to the Secretary of War, Edwin M. Stanton. But when approached with such a suggestion by a friend, Stanton told him bluntly, "Lincoln wrote it—every word of it. And he is capable of more than that."

In the hindsight of history, we can see that Stanton knew what he was talking about. But how was it that Lincoln turned out to be so exceptional a writer and that it was so little apparent to his contemporaries? Studying Lincoln's writing over the years has convinced me that most of the factors that contributed to Lincoln's extraordinary literary achievement were invisible to his public and were even contrary to its general sense of who he was. As a child, he was fascinated with words and meanings and obsessed with clarity, both in understanding and in being understood. He wrote all his life for local newspapers, although mostly anonymously, and harbored a lifelong tendency to meet provocation with a written response. By the 1850s, when he came to political prominence, he had already formed the habit of making notes on scraps of paper of ideas and phrases as they came to him, which he then used in composing speeches. Perhaps his most valuable and most unsuspected trait as a writer was his devotion to revision.

We know, of course, how it all turned out. Nowhere is that more evident than in the contrast between the two speeches given on Nov. 19, 1863. Everett, who had been a president of Harvard, a Congressman, a Senator and a Governor of Massachusetts as well as a Secretary of State and a minister to England, was chosen to deliver the principal address at the dedication of the new national cemetery on the battlefield at Gettysburg. Lincoln was invited almost as an afterthought. One man spoke for two hours, the other for two minutes. One speech was printed and distributed in advance and has rarely been read since. The other is one of the most famous compositions in the American language. ∎

Obsessed with clarity *At top left is the only photograph that shows Lincoln at Gettysburg. At right, Lincoln's 1862 letter to Horace Greeley is concise and plainspoken. The copy of the Gettysburg Address in Lincoln's hand is one of several he copied for posterity after giving the speech*

THE UNION AND SLAVERY.

Letter From the President to Horace Greeley.

EXECUTIVE MANSION,
WASHINGTON, Aug. 22, 1862.

Hon. Horace Greeley:

DEAR SIR: I have just read yours of the 19th, addressed to myself through the New-York Tribune. If there be in it any statements or assumptions of fact which I may know to be erroneous, I do not now and here controvert them. If there be in it any inferences which I may believe to be falsely drawn, I do not now and here argue against them. If there be perceptible in it an impatient and dictatorial tone, I waive it in deference to an old friend, whose heart I have always supposed to be right.

As to the policy I "seem to be pursuing," as you say, I have not meant to leave any one in doubt.

I would save the Union. I would save it the shortest way under the Constitution. The sooner the national authority can be restored the nearer the Union will be "the Union as it was." If there be those who would not save the Union unless they could at the same time *save* Slavery, I do not agree with them. If there be those who would not save the Union unless they could at the same time *destroy* Slavery, I do not agree with them. My paramount object in this struggle *is* to save the Union, and is *not* either to save or destroy Slavery. If I could save the Union without freeing *any* slave, I would do it, and if I could save it by freeing *all* the slaves, I would do it; and if I could save it by freeing some and leaving others alone, I would also do that. What I do about Slavery and the colored race, I do because I believe it helps to save this Union, and what I forbear, I forbear because I do *not* believe it would help to save the Union. I shall do *less* whenever I shall believe what I am doing hurts the cause, and I shall do *more* whenever I shall ——— will help the cause. I shall try to

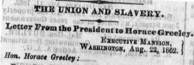

Executive Mansion,
Washington, , 186

Four score and seven years ago our fathers brought forth, upon this continent, a new nation, conceived in liberty, and dedicated to the proposition that "all men are created equal."

Now we are engaged in a great civil war, testing whether that nation, or any nation so conceived, and so dedicated, can long endure. We are met on a great battle field of that war. We have come to dedicate a portion of it, as a ——

"Every man is said to have his peculiar ambition. Whether it be true or not, I can say for one that I have no other so great as that of being truly esteemed of my fellow men, by rendering myself worthy of their esteem. How far I shall succeed in gratifying this ambition, is yet to be developed."

— EARLY POLITICAL SPEECH, MARCH 9, 1832

"Passion has helped us; but can do so no more. It will in future be our enemy. Reason—cold, calculating, unimpassioned reason—must furnish all the materials for our future support and defense."

— LYCEUM ADDRESS, SPRINGFIELD, JAN. 27, 1838

"In law it is a good policy to never plead what you need not, lest you oblige yourself to prove what you can not."

— LETTER TO USHER LINDER, FEB. 20, 1848

"Allow the President to invade a neighboring nation whenever he shall deem it necessary to repel an invasion and you allow him to do so whenever he may choose to say he deems it necessary for such purpose, and you allow him to make war at pleasure ... If today he should choose to say he thinks it necessary to invade Canada to prevent the British from invading us, how could you stop him? You may say to him, 'I see no probability of the British invading us,' but he will say to you, 'Be silent; I see it, if you don't.'"

— LETTER TO WILLIAM HERNDON, FEB. 15, 1848

"Slavery is founded in the selfishness of man's nature—opposition to it is in his love of justice. These principles are an eternal antagonism; and when brought into collision so fiercely, as slavery extension brings them, shocks, and throes, and convulsions must ceaselessly follow. Repeal the Missouri Compromise—repeal all compromises—repeal the Declaration of Independence—repeal all past history, you still can not repeal human nature. It still will be the abundance of man's heart, that slavery extension is wrong; and out of the abundance of his heart, his mouth will continue to speak."

— SPEECH AT PEORIA, OCT. 16, 1854

"This is a world of compensation; and he who would be no slave, must consent to have no slave. Those who deny freedom to others, deserve it not for themselves; and, under a just God, can not long retain it."

— LETTER TO HENRY PIERCE, APRIL 6, 1859

"The dogmas of the quiet past, are inadequate to the stormy present. The occasion is piled high with difficulty, and we must rise—with the occasion. As our case is new, so we must think anew, and act anew. We must disenthrall ourselves, and then we shall save our country.

"Fellow-citizens, we can not escape history. We of this Congress and this Administration will be remembered in spite of ourselves ... The fiery trial through which we pass will light us down in honor or dishonor to the latest generation ... In giving freedom to the slave we assure freedom to the free—honorable alike in what we give and what we preserve. We shall nobly save or meanly lose the last best hope of earth ... The way is plain, peaceful, generous, just—a way which if followed the world will forever applaud and God must forever bless."

— MESSAGE TO CONGRESS, DEC. 1, 1862

"And now, beware of rashness. Beware of rashness, but with energy, and sleepless vigilance, go forward, and give us victories."

— LETTER TO GENERAL JOSEPH HOOKER, JAN. 26, 1863

"The restoration of the Rebel States to the Union must rest upon the principle of civil and political equality of both races; and it must be sealed by general amnesty."

— LETTER TO JAMES S. WADSWORTH, JAN. 1864

"Nowhere in the world is presented a government of so much liberty and equality. To the humblest and poorest amongst us are held out the highest privileges and positions. The present moment finds me at the White House, yet there is as good a chance for your children as there was for my father's."

— SPEECH TO 148TH OHIO REGIMENT, AUG. 31, 1864

"Gen. Sheridan says 'If the thing is pressed I think that Lee will surrender.' Let the thing be pressed."

— LETTER TO GENERAL U.S. GRANT, APRIL 7, 1865

Wordsmith *This portrait of Lincoln at age 54 was taken by Alexander Gardner in 1863, the year Lincoln delivered his most enduring speech, the Gettysburg Address. Some of the quotations frequently attributed to Lincoln—including the famous chestnut about "fooling some of the people all of the time and all of the people some of the time"—are not accepted as verbatim by scholars*

"[Lincoln] was very indulgent to his children. He never neglected to praise them for any of their good acts. He often said, 'It is my pleasure that my children are free and happy, and unrestrained by parental tyranny. Love is the chain whereby to bind a child to its parents.'"

—MARY TODD LINCOLN, INTERVIEW WITH WILLIAM HERNDON, 1866

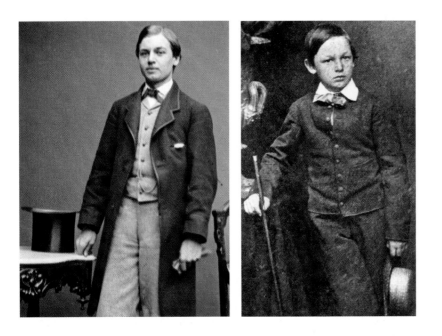

Hexed generation *Eldest son Robert, far left, was never close to his father and spent the war years at Harvard University. At near left is Willie Lincoln, a bright boy said to be his parents' favorite. His death early in 1862 plunged them into deep mourning.*

On the opposite page are Lincoln and Tad, who became very close after Willie's death. A lively lad with a mischievous streak, Tad had a speech impediment that made his words unintelligible to some, and he lagged in learning to read and write. Mary Todd's heart was broken again when he died from a mysterious "wasting disease" in 1871, at only 18. The family portrait below was painted in 1861 by Francis B. Carpenter

A Troubled Four Years in the White House

The Lincoln family moved into the White House, the nation's symbolic home, just as the nation was falling apart. The years that followed were as grim as the war over which Lincoln presided. There were moments of good cheer and laughter: Willie and Tad Lincoln were among the first children to occupy the White House, and they treated it like a giant playhouse, greeting visiting dignitaries by turning a fire hose on them. A captivated public showered them with gifts, including a pet goat for Tad. Mary Todd Lincoln busied herself with redecorating, but the First Lady was soon grief-stricken over the news that several Kentucky relatives had been killed in combat—fighting on the Confederate side. Her sadness was aggravated by her inability to grieve in public, lest she be accused of divided loyalties.

As the war grew ever bloodier, unrelenting scorn was heaped on Lincoln by his political foes, and the First Lady was also heavily criticized. In addition to being excoriated for exceeding the budget Congress had allotted for refurbishing the White House, she was lampooned for spending lavishly on her own wardrobe. And some in Washington looked down on the onetime Kentucky belle, calling her provincial. Sample comment from a Senator returning from a state dinner: "The weak minded Mrs. Lincoln had her bosom on exhibition, and a flower pot on her head."

Mary Lincoln was high-strung in the best of times, but her emotional state became more precarious in 1862, when Willie, much loved by his parents, died of typhoid fever at age 11. The First Lady took to holding séances in the White House, drawing new derision. And little was now denied their youngest son, Tad. He received a faux military commission from Secretary of War Edwin Stanton, along with a specially tailored, gold-braided uniform, and delighted in setting off a toy cannon at his father's office door during Cabinet meetings. As a 12th-birthday present, Lincoln took Tad with him to the fallen Confederate capital of Richmond, Va., on April 4, 1865, where the boy got to see his father mobbed by throngs of Union soldiers and freed slaves. Ten days later, it was Tad who tried to talk his father into accompanying him to Grover's Theater, for a production of *Aladdin and the Wonderful Lamp*—only to be overruled at the last minute by his mother: the senior Lincolns had already publicly committed to seeing a play at Ford's Theatre that night.

In the White House, Dreams Deferred

Mary Todd was a great believer in her husband's talents; as early as their courting days, she told friends that Abraham Lincoln would one day be President. But when the erstwhile Kentucky belle's vision of living in the White House was realized, both the national crisis and a series of personal tragedies conspired to make her time as First Lady seem more a nightmare than a dream.

At the Lincolns' first Inaugural Ball, in 1861, Mary made a splash in a beautiful blue dress and reminded guests of her intriguing background by dancing with her onetime beau, the powerful Senator Stephen A. Douglas. Finding the White House in a dreadful state when she moved in, Mary gave it a much needed top-to-bottom cleaning and furnished it lavishly—too lavishly. In shopping trips in Philadelphia and New York City in 1861, she badly overspent the $20,000 budget granted by Congress for White House furnishings. Her exasperated husband claimed he would refuse to ask Congress to appropriate extra monies for "flubdubs for that damned old house" during wartime, but in the end he did so.

On Feb. 5, 1862, the Lincolns hosted an elaborate reception to show off the newly refurbished mansion. The glittering event was a success, but when their third son, Willie, became ill and died shortly afterward, his grieving mother lost her delight in social affairs. She grew exasperated at having to open her home to the public for weekly receptions, during which some visitors snipped off swatches of drapes as souvenirs. The First Lady now turned to spiritualism and séances in hopes of communicating with her departed son.

On July 2, 1863, Mary was thrown from a runaway carriage—which may have been tampered with in hopes of injuring her husband—and suffered a head injury that became infected and magnified the pain of her recurring migraine headaches. Meanwhile, the war's divisions reverberated within her own family: three of her half-brothers were killed while fighting in Confederate uniform, leading Northern newspapers to question Mrs. Lincoln's sympathies. When her newly widowed half-sister Emilie Helm visited her at the White House in December 1863, the First Lady asked her, "Will we ever awake from this hideous nightmare?"

Receiving *Above, the Lincolns host the second Inaugural Ball in March 1865. The President greets a guest, with Mrs. Lincoln behind him and General Ulysses S. Grant on the right*

An Unusual First Friend

During her years in the White House, Mary Todd Lincoln's closest confidante was the fascinating Elizabeth Keckly, right, who served as Mrs. Lincoln's "modiste," or fashion adviser, and dressmaker. Keckly was a former slave whose father was her wealthy white owner; she endured years of physical and sexual abuse at the hands of white masters before managing to buy her freedom in 1855, thanks to her expertise as a dressmaker and enterprise as a businesswoman.

Keckly was introduced to Mrs. Lincoln by the wife of Senator Jefferson Davis, soon to become President of the Confederacy, on the day Lincoln was inaugurated. The two quickly became very close—Mary Todd Lincoln had grown up surrounded by black servants in a slaveholding Southern family—and Keckly became a familiar, daily presence in the White House, designing Mary's wardrobe and helping raise her young sons, Willie and Tad. After Lincoln's assassination, the two remained very close, for Mary had become dependent on Keckly's friendship and support. But when Keckly wrote a backstage memoir in 1868, *Behind the Scenes: Thirty Years a Slave and Four Years in the White House,* Mary considered it a betrayal and never spoke to her again. Keckly died in poverty in 1907, at age 88.

Finery and woe *Women followed styles in the mid-19th century in a host of magazines devoted to their concerns, including* Frank Leslie's Illustrated, *left, which displayed the fashionable dresses worn to the Lincolns' first Inaugural Ball, in 1861.*

Above, Mrs. Lincoln is shown in mourning attire after the death of son Willie in February 1862. The 1871 death of a third son, Tad, ushered in years of depression, illness and mental instability. She died in 1882, age 63.

The Saga of Mary Todd

Lincoln's wife was a full political partner. As **Walter Kirn** explains, that's one reason she was despised

FEW PATTERNS IN AMERICAN HISTORY have proved as durable as this one: while Presidents are attacked by their opponents for what they do or fail to do, First Ladies are disparaged for who they are. What's more, the unattractive traits that presidential spouses have been assigned don't seem to change. They're vain and frivolous (Jacqueline Kennedy in her designer gowns). Or they're pushy and calculating (Hillary Clinton and her failed health-care plan). Or they're irrational and superstitious (Nancy Reagan and her consulting astrologer).

Or they're all of the above—and loony too. That was Mary Todd Lincoln's uniquely miserable lot: to be despised in nearly every way that a First Lady is capable of being despised, both during her lifetime and ever since, while suffering in nearly every way that a human being can suffer. The fact that Mary was married to a President who has been admired in nearly every way that a President can be admired has never helped matters any. It may have sealed her fate.

"The most charitable construction that Mary Lincoln's friends can put on her strange course is that she is insane," wrote the Chicago *Journal* of the widow who, in the wake of her husband's assassination, had returned to Illinois in a state of conspicuous mourning that drew the opposite of public sympathy, particularly when she tried to raise money by selling off her fanciest clothes at auction. When Robert, the only one of her four sons whom she hadn't had to bury before his time, committed his aging mother to an asylum while taking control of her assets and affairs, Mary's humiliation was complete.

What did she do to deserve such vilification? As her modern biographers have pointed out, Mary Todd Lincoln's greatest sin, perhaps, was to be born in the wrong century. The daughter of a prominent Kentucky family whose mother died when she was just a girl, Mary was a bright, well-educated woman who dared to involve herself in her husband's political career. In 1847, when Abraham Lincoln trav-

Strawberry field *Mary Todd Lincoln enjoyed the social aspects of being First Lady. She posed for Mathew Brady in 1861 in an elaborate dress with a strawberry pattern, top left, that is now part of the collection of the Lincoln Presidential Library in Springfield, Ill.*

Nov 2d.

My Dear Husband
I have waited in vain to hear from you, yet as you are not given to letter writing, will be charitable enough to impute your silence, to the right cause. Strangers come up from W— & tell me you are well— which satisfies me very much— Your name is on every lip and many prayers and good wishes are hourly sent up, for your welfare— And McClellan + his slowness are as vehemently discussed, Allowing this beautiful weather, to pass away, is disheartening the North—

First counsellor *In the note at left, which seems awkwardly formal to modern ears, the President's wife advises her husband on how to deal with the recalcitrant General George McClellan. Above, the china Mary bought for the White House; she schemed to keep Lincoln unaware of her expenditures*

eled to Washington to take his seat as a newly elected Illinois Congressman, Mary had the presumption to accompany him—an unusual move for a political wife back then. She was on a mission, though. Having already tutored her mate in the fine points of proper manners and dress ("I do not think he knew pink from blue when I married him," she once told her sister), she made no secret of her ambition to see him ascend to the presidency one day. Later, during Lincoln's unsuccessful campaign for the Senate, Mary monitored his treatment by the press, lobbied on his behalf and cheered him on during his last public skirmish with Stephen Douglas, one of her rejected romantic suitors.

Once the Lincolns relocated to the White House, Mary made a grievous public-relations error that later First Ladies such as Nancy Reagan might have been wise to remember: she redecorated, expensively, extensively and—in the eyes of many—frivolously. Despite a historical catastrophe (the Civil War), Mary dedicated her formidable energies to buying china, ordering wallpaper, updating her wardrobe and bringing good taste and material splendor to a dowdy, poorly maintained residence whose appearance a White House secretary compared to that of "an old and unsuccessful hotel."

But America wasn't ready for Camelot, and Mary was cast as an out-of-touch princess who picked fabric swatches while, on the battlefield, the Republic burned. Yet perhaps no woman in American history had a better excuse for trying to boost her mood with a little retail therapy. Mary had already lost a mother and a son, and was about to lose another son, as well as her husband. She seemed to know that too, possibly as a result of her excursions into the mysterious spirit world, a popular pastime in the traumatized living rooms of the Civil War. Seeking comfort wherever she could find it, Mary switched off the lights and called her period's version of a psychic hotline.

Smart, ambitious women who love to shop, have difficulty sticking to a budget and react to emotional upheaval by dabbling in New Age spirituality don't attract much attention nowadays. If eventually they become fond of prescription medications, as her best modern biographer Jean H. Baker believes that Mary did (thereby clearing the way for Betty Ford), they may even have a rehab center named after them.

Mary Todd Lincoln had no such luck, though—except, of course, to become the negative role model for every First Lady ever since and also, perhaps, for the First Husbands of tomorrow. If Mary's tortured ghost (and she believed in ghosts—they were among her only companions at the end) could offer those First Spouses any advice, it might come down to this: Stay in the background, avoid having your fortune told and don't—at least not before speaking to your spouse—purchase new clothes or change the White House wallpaper. Your nation may soften its view of you someday, but it could take a long, long time. ∎

Walter Kirn is a novelist, critic and journalist who is a contributing editor of TIME

The Sioux Uprising, 1862

Lincoln's time in office was so dominated by the Civil War that it's easy to overlook other events and initiatives of his presidency. One of his challenges had preoccupied every President from Washington on: the relationship of the expanding U.S. with the nation's Native Americans. Lincoln was no stranger to this vexing problem: his grandfather, also named Abraham, had been slain by Indians, and Lincoln had served in the Black Hawk War of 1832. Now, 30 years later, Lincoln was again plunged into this long-running fray.

On Aug. 17, 1862, a hunting party of four Sioux Indians left their reservation in the Dakota Territory, crossed into the new state of Minnesota (admitted to the Union in 1858) and killed five white settlers. The Indians were justifiably angry over delayed payment of annuities promised them by the U.S. for agreeing to move to reserved land in the territory. When settlers retaliated, full-scale war broke out in the Minnesota River Valley. Lincoln sent General John Pope, who had walked into a trap in the Union loss at the Second Battle of Bull Run, to take command of an enlarged U.S. Army force in the region, and on Sept. 23, Pope led a battle in which entrenched Sioux were routed by superior numbers and more powerful arms.

The uprising was over, but Minnesota whites now demanded that more than 300 captured Sioux warriors be put to death. The President may have shared much of the pervasive racism of his time, but he had a very keen sense of justice, and he dug in his heels. Even while consumed by the urgencies of the war, Lincoln personally reviewed the charges against every Indian condemned to death by U.S. military tribunals and reduced the number of those to be hanged to 38—still the largest mass execution in U.S. history. When told his decision would cost him the support of white settlers clamoring for blood, Lincoln replied that he would not hang innocent men for votes.

Prairie showdown
Above, settlers fleeing the Sioux rest on the plain; more than 100 whites, mainly women and children, were taken captive during the conflict but most of them survived. Below, a delegation of Indians visits the White House, where Lincoln gave them a cordial, if paternalistic, reception

Amid War, a Progressive Political Agenda

Lincoln's legacy is defined by his success in saving the Union and helping end slavery in America. But the politics of wartime also helped him achieve many of the goals he had first espoused as a young Whig legislator in the 1830s. One of Lincoln's greatest political setbacks—and there are many to choose from—occurred when the idealistic program of state investments in roads, canals and bridges he supported in Illinois came a cropper in 1837, the victim of a nationwide financial panic. Now, as President, he presided over a U.S. Congress controlled by Republicans, many of them former Whigs, while many Democrats who opposed such policies were now Confederates.

With Republicans in command, Congress now passed, and Lincoln approved, some of the most progressive legislation in the nation's young history. On May 20, 1862, the President signed into law the Homestead Act, which awarded 160 acres of federal land to a registered applicant who pledged to improve it. Long opposed by Southerners who feared homesteading might rival the plantation economy, the act eventually resulted in the settling of some 1.6 million homesteads on the frontier. Lincoln and Congress also took lasting measures to improve education and make learning more affordable to all—a goal understandably close to Lincoln's heart—by chartering a series of land-grant universities, transforming higher education in America. The 37th Congress, sitting in 1861-63, also passed the Pacific Railway Act, chartering a transcontinental railroad and telegraph, and the National Banking Act, which made U.S. currency uniform for the first time. Lincoln's achievements as one of the most progressive chief executives in U.S. history are an unsung aspect of his presidency.

Ever so humble
Thomas Jefferson, who stepped down from the presidency in 1809, the year Lincoln was born, dreamed of an America populated by civic-minded farmers. With the Louisiana Purchase in 1803, he acquired the land to make that dream a reality. The Homestead Act of 1862 was another giant step that helped millions of settlers, like these farmers in Custer County, Nebraska, circa 1870, become landowners

"Truth constrains us to say that 'Honest Abe' is not a handsome man, but he is not so ill-looking as he has been represented. 'Handsome is that handsome does,' however, is a sensible adage."

—THE NEW YORK *TRIBUNE*, 1860

"A horrid-looking wretch he is, sooty and scoundrelly in aspect, a cross between the nutmeg dealer, the horse swapper, and the night man, a creature 'fit evidently for petty treason, small stratagems, and all sorts of spoils.' He is a lank-sided Yankee of the uncomeliest visage, and of the dirtiest complexion. Faugh! After him what decent white man would be President?"

—THE CHARLESTON *MERCURY*, JUNE 9, 1860

"Lincoln is is the leanest, lankest, most ungainly mass of legs and arms and hatchet face ever strung on a single frame."

—HOUSTON *TELEGRAPH*, 1860

"Something about the man, the face, is unfathomable. In his looks there were hints of mysteries within."

—LINCOLN'S FRIEND GUSTAVE KOERNER, IN AN UNDATED LETTER, PROBABLY FROM 1860

"I went to the White House shortly after tea where I found 'the original gorilla,' about as intelligent as ever. What a specimen to be at the head of our affairs now!"

—GENERAL GEORGE MCCLELLAN, IN A LETTER TO HIS WIFE, NOV. 17, 1861

"To say that he is ugly is nothing; to add that his figure is grotesque, is to convey no adequate impression. Fancy a man 6 feet high and thin out of proportion ... with a long scraggy neck, and a chest too narrow for the great arms at his side. Add to this figure a head, coconut-shaped and somewhat too small for such a stature, covered with rough uncombed and uncombable hair, that stands out in every direction at once: a face furrowed, wrinkled and indented as though it had been scarred by vitriol: a high narrow forehead, and sunk deep beneath bushy eyebrows; two bright, somewhat dreamy eyes that seem to gaze through you without looking at you; a few irregular blotches of black, bristly hair in the place where beard and whiskers

ought to grow; a close-set, thin lipped, stern mouth, with two rows of large, white teeth and a nose and ears which have been taken by mistake from a head of twice the size ... Add to all of this an air of strength, physical as well as moral, and a strange look of dignity coupled with all this grotesqueness, and you will have the impression left upon me by Abraham Lincoln."

—NEW YORK *SUNDAY MERCURY*, JUNE 1, 1862

"Lincoln is a sui generis figure in the annals of history ... He gives his most important actions always the most commonplace form ... He sings the bravura aria of his part hesitantly, reluctantly and unwillingly, as though apologising for being compelled by circumstances 'to act the lion.'"

—KARL MARX, OCT. 7, 1862

"He impressed me as being just what every one of you have been in the habit of calling him—an honest man. I never met with a man, who, on the first blush, impressed me more entirely with his sincerity, with his devotion to his country, and with his determination to save it at all hazards."

—FREDERICK DOUGLASS, SPEECH TO THE AMERICAN ANTI-SLAVERY SOCIETY, PHILADELPHIA, DECEMBER 1863

"He has a face like a hoosier Michael Angelo, so awful ugly it becomes beautiful, with its strange mouth, its deep-cut, criss-cross lines, and its doughnut complexion."

—WALT WHITMAN, UNDATED LETTER TO NATHANIEL BLOOM AND JOHN F.S. GRAY, 1863

"... He was odd, angular, homely, but when those little gray eyes and face were lighted up by the inward soul on fires of emotion ... then it was that all those apparently ugly or homely features sprang into organs of beauty. Sometimes it did appear to me that Lincoln was just fresh from the presence and hands of his creator."

—WILLIAM HERNDON, PUBLIC LECTURE, SPRINGFIELD, DECEMBER 1865

OLD ABE—" *Oh, it's all well enough to say, that I must support the dignity of my high office by Force—but it's darned uncomfortable sitting—I can tell yer.*"

Skewered *This political cartoon appeared in March 1861, shortly after Lincoln was inaugurated, when he was forced to decide whether to attempt to relieve federal troops holding Fort Sumter in Charleston Harbor, already under siege by South Carolina state militia. During his national career, critics assailed Lincoln's looks, his size and his frontier manners and speech*

117

THE COPPERHEAD PARTY.——IN FAVOR OF *A VIGOROUS PROSECUTION OF PEACE!*

Lincoln's Battlefields in the North

Not all of Lincoln's battles were military: he called opposition to the Civil War in the North "the fire in the rear." Northern Democrats who opposed the war were known derisively as "Copperheads," after the poisonous snake that strikes without warning. Their ranks included Congressmen, clerics, academics, journalists and politicians, and they showed the breadth of the support for their cause when Republicans who supported Lincoln were defeated throughout the North in the 1862 midterm elections. As war casualties mounted, a faction of extreme Copperheads not only fought Lincoln's policies but also courted subversion: they actively interfered with Army recruiting, encouraged desertion and incited riots in New York City and other cites. Some peace activists even conspired unsuccessfully with Confederate agents to raise armed resistance to the war in the North.

To fight his opponents—skewered above in a magazine cartoon—Lincoln came as close as any U.S. President ever has to the status of dictator. Employing measures that remain highly controversial, he sometimes suspended the right of habeas corpus, allowed trials of civilians by military tribunals, selectively imposed martial law and in some cases suppressed newspapers and interdicted mail. At times, more than 10,000 people were detained on suspicion of disloyalty. In 1863 the leader of the extreme Copperheads, Ohio Congressman Clement Vallandigham, was arrested by the Army and sentenced to prison for the remainder of the war. To avoid turning his nemesis into a martyr, Lincoln allowed him to slip away quietly to Canada.

Lincoln's fears peaked as the 1864 elections approached. After a summer of major Union defeats, the Democrats chose the popular General George McClellan *(inset)* to run against the President who had downgraded him, and Lincoln believed he would not be re-elected. But the tide turned early in the fall, thanks to the force of arms rather than the suppression of dissent: a series of victories at Mobile Bay, Atlanta and the Shenandoah Valley drove Northern public opinion back in favor of the war, and Lincoln was re-elected by a landslide.

A close call *The Union came very close to an outright war with Britain late in 1861, when the U.S.S.* San Jacinto *intercepted the British mail packet RMS* Trent *and arrested two Southern diplomats, above, bound for England to seek diplomatic recognition for the Confederacy. Lincoln soon released the two and disavowed the actions of Union Captain Charles Wilkes*

Across the Ocean, Dangerous Sympathies

A source of major concern for Lincoln—and of perpetual hope for the South—was that Britain or France might actively intervene in the war by taking the side of the Confederacy. The danger was magnified by Britain's dependence on cheap Southern cotton to keep its booming Industrial Revolution running, and by the leanings of its conservative aristocrats, who shared the South's attachment to social hierarchies. While there seemed little danger of outright military assistance, such as France had offered the American colonies during the Revolutionary War, Lincoln feared that the European powers might strike trade and supply agreements with the Confederacy that would break the Union blockade of Southern ports. Even the simple act of extending diplomatic recognition would have offered crucial support to the besieged South, amounting to a recognition of its status as an independent nation rather than a rebellious region.

"There is here, as there has always been, one political power, namely, the United States of America, competent to make war and peace, and conduct commerce and alliances with all foreign nations," Lincoln and his Secretary of State, William Seward, wrote to European capitals shortly after the fall of Fort Sumter in 1861. But as long as the war remained undecided, so did the European powers, despite the strong efforts of the able Union diplomat in London, Charles Francis Adams of the notable Massachusetts family *(inset)*. In August 1862, after the Union defeat at the Second Battle of Bull Run, British P.M. Henry Temple (Lord Palmerston) pondered an alliance with the South, saying, "if the Federals sustain [another] great defeat … their Cause will be manifestly hopeless … and the iron should be struck while it is hot." A few weeks later, Southern losses at Antietam changed his mind. Ultimately, the inability of the South to win conclusive victories convinced Palmerston (whose lead France was sure to follow) that Europeans "must be on-lookers until the war should have taken a more decided turn." When it finally did, in the fall of 1864, that turn was in favor of the North.

WHAT LINCOLN SAID

"With malice toward none; with charity for all; with firmness in the right, as God gives us to see the right, let us strive on to finish the work we are now in; to bind up the nation's wounds; to care for him who shall have borne the battle, and for his widow, and his orphan—to do all which may achieve and cherish a just and lasting peace, among ourselves, and with all nations."

Unfinished Business

In April 1864 the nation entered the fourth year of civil war. The conflict had another full year to run—and might have run longer had Lincoln not made a key decision in March, 1864: he placed Ulysses S. Grant in command of all Union armies. Though Grant would commit some deadly errors in the months that followed, with his accession to supreme command, the end of the war may be said to have begun.

Lincoln also faced a reckoning; 1864 was an election year, and he faced challenges from within his own party. Thanks to adroit political maneuverings—an aspect of Lincoln's character often overlooked by his idolaters— the President systematically removed the barriers to his nomination. He outflanked Radicals on the party's left and "war Democrats" on the right who opposed his conduct of the conflict, and he dispatched his ambitious Cabinet member, Salmon P. Chase, to the Supreme Court. Lincoln easily won the nomination at the Republican Convention in Baltimore early in June, where the party adopted a platform calling for a constitutional amendment to outlaw slavery and named Tennessee Senator Andrew Johnson as Lincoln's running mate. It also adopted a new name: to cast a wide net for voters, Lincoln ran under the banner of the National Union party.

The Democrats' nominee, General George B. McClellan, was hampered by the party's platform, which called for reaching the earliest possible peace with the South, thus allowing the Confederacy, and slavery, to stand. With many Northerners heartily sick of the meat-grinding war, Lincoln began to fear he would lose as the summer dragged on. But when General William T. Sherman's army captured Atlanta on Sept. 2, Northern hearts—and Lincoln's chances—soared. On Nov. 8, Lincoln won a massive victory, carrying all but three states and winning 212 electoral votes to McClellan's 21.

By Inauguration Day, March 4, Northern advances made clear that the war would soon be over. Looking ahead, Lincoln delivered a speech that bears comparison to his remarks at Gettysburg. Refusing to malign the South, he noted that all Americans were complicit in the sins of slavery and called for the nation to move forward "with malice toward none; with charity for all." One attendee, journalist Noah Brooks, reported that as Lincoln stood up to speak, the sun burst through a layer of clouds and "flooded the spectacle with glory and light." When he saw the President the next day, said Brooks, Lincoln remarked, "Did you notice that sunburst? It made my heart jump."

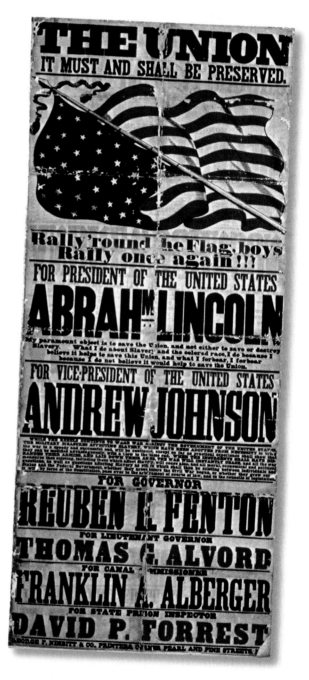

Second term *Above, an 1864 campaign poster supports National Union (Republican) candidates in New York. At left, Lincoln delivers his second inaugural address at the Capitol. Among those listening: John Wilkes Booth*

Making—and Unmaking—Tracks

"To realize what war is," General William Tecumseh Sherman wrote to his wife in 1863, "one must follow our tracks … We have devoured the land. All the people retire before us, and desolation is behind." A pioneer of the concept of "total war," Sherman was determined to destroy not only any military target he could lay his hands on but also the economic sinews that enabled Confederates to wage war—as well as the will of Southern civilians to support it. Late in 1864, Sherman's troops cut a swath across Georgia, destroying railroads (as in Atlanta, above) as well as bridges, factories, farms (including livestock, crops and wells) and entire cities—Atlanta was burned to the ground on Nov. 15, by Union troops departing for Savannah. During the month-long "march to the sea" that followed, they laid waste to thousands of square miles of Southern territory. At top are the notes in which Sherman presented Lincoln with a Christmas gift—the city of Savannah—and the President congratulated him.

Even as Sherman was advancing on Atlanta, Union General Philip Sheridan was capturing the Shenandoah Valley, "the breadbasket of the Confederacy" and one of the last sources of provisions for the armies of the South. When he was through, Sheridan bragged that "a crow flying over the Shenandoah Valley would be well advised to carry its own provisions." The Union pincers were closing around Robert E. Lee's Army of Northern Virginia.

122

In Victory, Magnanimity

After reaching Savannah and the Atlantic Ocean, General Sherman hooked left and began marching northward (torching Columbia, S.C., as he went), toward the rear of Robert E. Lee's position at the railroad junction of Petersburg, Va., where the Southern general had been faced off in a stalemate against Ulysses S. Grant's troops for nine months. Commanding soldiers on the brink of starvation, facing an unbreakable line in front of him and now vulnerable to attack from the rear, Lee had no avenue of retreat. Escape to the east was cut off by the Atlantic Ocean; escape to the west was cut off by Sheridan's advancing army. On the night of April 2, Lee withdrew from Petersburg, at the same time advising Confederate president Jefferson Davis to leave Richmond, which he did. Union troops occupied both Petersburg and Richmond the next day. Grant immediately set out in pursuit of Lee.

Now surrounded, Lee accepted the inevitable and requested a meeting with Grant. On April 9, in the village of Appomattox Court House (above), Lee surrendered and Grant wrote out by hand the generous terms devised by Lincoln: "officers and men paroled … arms and matériel surrendered … not to include officer's side-arms … let all men who claim to own a horse or mule take the animals home with them." As Lee departed, a few Union soldiers erupted in cheers; Grant stopped them with the words "The rebels are our countrymen again."

Fall of the South

Robert E. Lee's withdrawal from Petersburg, Va., ensured that Richmond would be overrun by Northern troops. The Confederate capital fell on April 3, only hours after President Jefferson Davis fled—first to southern Virginia, then to North Carolina. Within 24 hours, Lincoln made an impulsive decision: he toured Richmond with his son Tad while it was still smoldering from Union cannon barrages. The President was thronged by admiring blacks and hailed by Union troops; he also visited the Confederate White House, where he sat in Davis' chair.

The news that Richmond had fallen and Lee had surrendered unleashed a wave of giddy excitement in Northern cities. On the evening of April 11, with the Union victory secured, the nation's capital was illuminated and a festive crowd gathered on the White House lawn, clamoring to cheer the President. Lincoln appeared at a second-floor window above the North Portico to address the revelers. But if the crowd was hoping to hear the victor gloat or promise retribution, they were disappointed. Returning to his theme of forgiveness and reconciliation, he urged his listeners to welcome the Southern states back into the fold without divisive argument over their behavior, indeed, "without deciding, or even considering, whether these States have ever been out of the Union, than with it. Finding themselves safely at home, it would be utterly immaterial whether they had ever been abroad."

After concluding his remarks, the President struck another surprisingly conciliatory note: he stunned the crowd by asking the band to strike up *Dixie*, which he called "one of the best tunes I have ever heard." At least one member of the crowd was unmoved by Lincoln's magnanimous gesture, however: glaring at the speaker and scheming in the darkness stood the man who had been shadowing Lincoln for weeks, the actor John Wilkes Booth.

Harvest of War *Fires sprang up throughout Richmond on the night Confederate leaders fled and Union troops entered the city; entire sections burned to the ground*

Murder at the Theater

As an itinerant actor, John Wilkes Booth had no regular address, so he was in the habit of receiving mail at theaters where he frequently played. Stopping at Ford's Theatre in Washington for this reason on April 14, he learned that Abraham Lincoln was scheduled to be in the audience that night. Over the next few hours, Booth, 26—a Southern sympathizer who had conspired amateurishly for more than a year to kidnap the President but had never attempted to implement his plans—feverishly contacted his henchmen and set in motion a haphazard plot to kill not only Lincoln but also Vice President Andrew Johnson, General Ulysses S. Grant and Secretary of State William Seward.

Booth easily gained entrance to the theater that evening; with a good deal of luck he also slipped by the President's careless security detail. As the audience enjoyed the farce *Our American Cousin*, the seasoned actor waited for what he knew to be the play's biggest laugh line, as the American rube, Dundreary, calls after his snooty British relative: "Well, I guess I know enough to turn you inside out, old gal—you sockdologizing old man-trap."

Booth used the crowd's roar to cloak the sound as he turned the doorknob of the President's box. He stepped quietly behind Lincoln and aimed his single-shot derringer, point blank, behind the President's left ear. The peals of laughter were still echoing as Booth fired, sending a .44-cal. bullet tearing diagonally through Lincoln's brain. As the President slumped forward, Booth leapt from the balcony onto the stage, badly injuring his leg in the process. Some in the audience would remember Booth as quoting the motto of Virginia, *Sic semper tyrannis* (Thus always to tyrants) as he fled; others recalled him shouting "The South is avenged!" Elsewhere, Booth's fellow plotters failed in their deadly tasks. Confederate spy Lewis Powell talked his way into Seward's home and brutally stabbed the Secretary, but he survived. Grant had suddenly left town, and hired gun George Atzerodt apparently drank himself into a stupor rather than trying to kill Johnson.

Lincoln was taken to a boarding house across the street from Ford's Theatre, but he never regained consciousness and doctors could do nothing for him. The 16th President of the United States died at 7:22 a.m. the following morning.

CONTEMPORARY VOICES

"The exultation of victory over the final and successful triumph of Union arms was suddenly changed to the lamentations of grief... The public heart, filled with joy over the news from Appomattox, now sank low with a sacred terror as the sad tidings from the Capitol came in."

—WILLIAM HERNDON

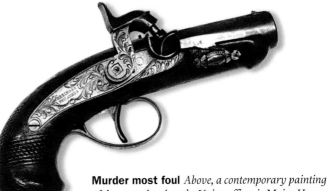

Murder most foul *Above, a contemporary painting of the assassination; the Union officer is Major Henry Rathbone. His fiancé, Clara Harris, is seated next to Mrs. Lincoln. Booth's derringer is in the collection of Ford's Theatre. At top left, the playhouse was draped in crepe following the assassination. The playbill below lists the evening's entertainment*

127

The Price of Homicide

It took less than two weeks to round up most of those suspected of complicity in the murder of Lincoln. Twelve days after the assassination, John Wilkes Booth and co-conspirator David Herold, a pharmacist who had accompanied Lewis Powell to the home of Secretary of State William Seward on April 12, were surrounded by Union troops in a barn near Port Royal, Va. Herold surrendered, but Booth opted for what he hoped would be a heroic last stand: he remained inside while his pursuers set fire to the barn and then shot him through the neck. "Tell Mother I died for my country," he said to the soldiers, then looked down at his now paralyzed hands and muttered "useless, useless" before dying.

Herold was imprisoned with the other plotters arrested days earlier: gunman George Atzerodt (who had reneged on his vow to kill Vice President Andrew Johnson), Lewis Powell (the Confederate spy who stabbed but failed to kill Seward) and Mary Surrat (mother of conspirator John Surrat, at whose tavern Booth and Herold stopped before fleeing South on the night of Lincoln's murder).

On May 1, 1865, President Johnson ordered an Army tribunal to judge whether the four had "maliciously, unlawfully, and traitorously" conspired to murder Lincoln and others. The trials ended on June 29, after the testimony of more than 300 witnesses was heard. On July 5, the court rendered its verdict: all four were convicted and sentenced to death. Four other defendants, including Dr. Samuel Mudd, who had treated Booth's broken leg, were sentenced to jail terms ranging from six years to life.

Two days later, Surrat, Atzerodt, Powell and Herold were led through the prison yard at Fort McNair in Washington, past four freshly dug graves, each with a pine ammunition crate that would serve as a coffin beside it; they climbed a gallows and were hanged. Their bodies were allowed to dangle for 20 minutes—perhaps for the benefit of photographers—before they were cut down and quickly buried.

"I told [John Wilkes Booth, who was surrounded in a Virginia barn] I had not come to fight; that I had 50 men, and could take him. Then he said, 'Well, my brave boys, prepare me a stretcher, and place another stain on our glorious banner.'"

—ACCOUNT OF LIEUTENANT EDWARD DOHERTY, LEADER OF THE UNION DETAIL THAT CAPTURED BOOTH

Death penalty *Above, four of the conspirators in Lincoln's murder are hanged. Booth, shown at left in an undated photo, eluded a massive manhunt for 12 days, while posters like the one at top left were placed throughout Maryland, Virginia and the District of Columbia. Booth's older brother Edwin, the noted Shakespearean actor, was able to continue his career despite the ignominy attached to his name*

A Nation in Mourning

Abraham Lincoln left Washington, D.C., the way he had arrived: his remains traveled by train along the same route he had taken from Illinois to the capital in 1861 as President-elect. Edwin Stanton, in charge of the arrangements, believed the long memorial tour would help vent Northern anger at the assassination and allow the nation some measure of finality in its initial experience of collective grief. Lincoln was America's first leader to be assassinated—his murder, it was widely noted, occurred on Good Friday—and his transformation from complicated man to venerated icon was completed well before he was interred.

The two-week trip covered some 1,600 miles, during which more than 1 million people paid their respects. Preceded by a "pilot" locomotive draped in black crepe that would serve to alert mourners as Lincoln's cortege approached, the eight-car train carried more than 300 mourners as it left Washington on April 21. The train moved north through Maryland, Pennsylvania and New York before hooking west to Ohio, Indiana and Illinois. Stopping in 20 cities, it was greeted everywhere by delegations of local dignitaries, military and police honor guards and legions of common people. In Lancaster, Pa., an old man in a carriage watched from the edge of the crowd as the train passed: few recognized him as James Buchanan, Lincoln's predecessor. Stopping in 20 cities, the President's casket was removed and escorted to a place of honor (usually a courthouse or other government building) where it would lie in state for a few hours for public viewing before it was taken back aboard the train to resume its journey.

Lincoln's oldest son Robert represented the family; the train also carried the body of his deceased brother Willie, who was accompanying his father to Illinois for reburial. Lincoln's widow was too distraught to endure either the train ride or the funeral; younger son Tad remained with her.

In Springfield the casket was transferred to a special hearse, finished in gold, silver and crystal, that had been shipped from St. Louis. It was escorted by so many mourners that the back of the procession didn't arrive at the grave site until hours after the funeral was over. Many months would pass before Mary Todd Lincoln could bear to visit the magnificent tomb that housed her husband and son. Then, overcome with grief, she left quickly and never returned to the site.

Philadelphia

Chicago

Pilot locomotive

New York

THE NATION MOURNS.

Springfield

Last rites *The nation's mourning was extravagant, and can be seen as an expression of sorrow at the war's cost as well as at Lincoln's murder. Though Mary Todd Lincoln did not join the railroad memorial journey or attend her husband's funeral, her will was nonetheless felt: when Illinois politicians began arguing that Lincoln should be buried on the grounds of the state capital, she threatened to send his remains back to Washington. They hastily agreed to inter Lincoln at Springfield's Oak Ridge Cemetery (which he had helped dedicate in 1859), as she demanded*

Lincoln's casket

Marian Anderson 1939

Nikita Khrushchev 1959

Lincoln in the American Memory

Lincoln may have been laid to rest in Springfield in 1865, but his spirit still looms large in the American imagination. Soon after his death, admirers began urging that a monument be erected to the slain President. As always, Washington made haste slowly: the Lincoln Memorial was opened in 1922, 57 years after he was assassinated. Designed by Henry Bacon along classical lines, the structure might have pleased Lincoln, who worked through all of Euclid's books on geometry in his 40s as he rode the circuit of county courthouses in Illinois. And Daniel Chester French's seated statue of Lincoln is powerfully grand. But you don't have to know much about Lincoln to know he would have been acutely embarrassed at his elevation into a semi-divinity and would likely have dug out a homely story to mock himself and hide his chagrin.

No matter: the memorial is for us, not him. We need him. Leo Tolstoy, Karl Marx, Theodore Roosevelt, Ho Chi Minh, Mohandas Gandhi, Ronald Reagan, Nelson Mandela: all admired him. Even Nikita Khrushchev and a young Fidel Castro paid their respects at the memorial.

Lincoln's ideals still resonate, drawing protesters and Presidents. Marian Anderson sang here in 1939 when Jim Crow segregation kept her from performing at a nearby recital hall. The Rev. Martin Luther King Jr. spoke here in 1963, urging America to pay off the "promissory note" of equal rights for all that Lincoln left the nation. In a seldom-recalled story, President Richard Nixon came here in May 1970, just before dawn, to meet with college students protesting the U.S. invasion of Cambodia; perhaps he was searching for Lincoln's mantle.

That mantle, as Lincoln would have understood, is more enduring than marble: it's in the words he spoke, chiseled onto the memorial's walls. It is their power that keeps Lincoln's spirit always alive in our imaginations. When America's house is divided, they urge us to bind up the nation's wounds, and to do so with malice toward none and charity for all. In our darkest hours, they ask us to re-dedicate ourselves to a new birth of freedom, so that government of the people, by the people and—well, you know the rest. And that's why Lincoln still lives.

132

Lincoln Memorial

Fidel Castro 1959

WHAT LINCOLN SAID

"Whenever I hear any one arguing for slavery, I feel a strong impulse to see it tried on him personally."

—ADDRESS TO UNION
SOLDIERS, MARCH 17, 1865

Martin Luther King Jr. 1963

For Further Reading

Lincoln
David Herbert Donald
Simon & Schuster; 1995

This comprehensive biography by a Harvard historian and leading Lincoln scholar is a highly readable and rewarding one-volume introduction to Lincoln's life and times.

The Lincolns: Portrait of a Marriage
Daniel Mark Epstein
Ballantine Books; 2008

Poet and biographer Epstein studies the Lincolns' married life, arguing that they were deeply in love, giving new credit to Mary as a full political partner of her husband's and dispelling notions that Mary was a lunatic and Abe a saint.

Land of Lincoln
Andrew Ferguson
Grove Press; 2007 (Paperback)

Ferguson, an editor at *The Weekly Standard*, travels the country to train an acerbic, illuminating eye on the many ways in which modern America remembers Lincoln, from high-tech museums to executive retreats at Gettysburg. Bright, brisk and enjoyable.

Team of Rivals: The Political Genius of Abraham Lincoln
Doris Kearns Goodwin
Simon & Schuster; 2005

The acclaimed biographer, who contributed the article "Master of the Game" to this volume, exam-ines Lincoln through the prism of his relations with his Cabinet members, offering us a new way to appreciate both the difficulties he overcame and his often overlooked abilities as a student of character and politics.

Herndon's Lincoln: The True Story of a Great Life
William Herndon and Jesse W. Weik
University of Illinois Press; 2006

This fascinating biography is required reading for anyone interested in Lincoln, yet it is surprisingly little known to general readers. The University of Illinois Press edition, prepared by Douglas O. Wilson and Rodney Davis, directors of the Knox College Lincoln Studies Center, is the place to start. Lincoln's longtime friend and law partner may be said to have originated the "oral history" format with this volume, interviewing and corresponding with Lincoln's early friends and acquaintances to present "the whole truth concerning him." The volume is shot through with Herndon's personal opinions and preferences. (Don't trust him on Mary Todd.)

Abraham Lincoln: Speeches and Writings, 1832-1858
Abraham Lincoln: Speeches and Writings, 1859-1865
Library of America; 1989

There's no substitute for Lincoln

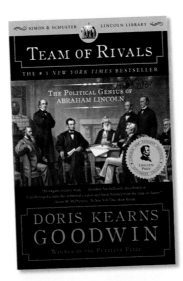

taken straight-up. A gold mine for browsers, students and Lincoln fans.

Lincoln's Melancholy: How Depression Challenged a President and Fueled His Greatness
Joshua Wolf Shenk
Houghton Miflin; 2005

Lincoln's life has been probed from just about every angle, but Shenk uncovers fertile new ground by exploring Lincoln's habitual melancholy and bouts of depression, aspects of his character familiar to contemporaries but often ignored or pushed into the background in recent times.

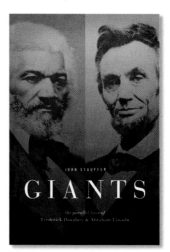

Giants: The Parallel Lives of Frederick Douglass & Abraham Lincoln
John Stauffer
Twelve; 2008

The Harvard professor who wrote "The Great Divide" article in this volume strikes sparks with this dual biography of Lincoln and Douglass, shedding light on two towering figures of the 19th century.

Lincoln's Sword: The Presidency and the Power of Words
Douglas L. Wilson
Alfred A. Knopf; 2006

Wilson, a noted scholar who wrote the article on Lincoln's prose style in this volume, examines the roots of his strengths as writer and orator.

Abraham Lincoln Presidential Library and Museum
Springfield, Ill.

This popular complex includes the Lincoln Library, which opened in 2004, and a separate museum that opened in 2005. The museum's high-tech, immersive visual presentations have been a hit with tourists but have also been derided by some scholars and guests as superficial. Either way, the collection of Lincoln memorabilia in the complex is unsurpassed.

Other Springfield Historical Sites
Springfield, Ill.

In addition to the Presidential Library and Museum, the Illinois capital contains several other significant sites that welcome tourists, including the Lincoln Home; the Old State Capitol Building, where Lincoln delivered the "House Divided" speech; the Lincoln Tomb; the Lincoln-Herndon Law Office; and the Lincoln Depot, scene of the 1861 Farewell Address.

Lincoln's New Salem State Historic Site
New Salem, Ill. (20 miles northwest of Springfield)

The small pioneer village where Lincoln spent his young adulthood was completely abandoned in his own lifetime, but has been restored as a historical site that seeks to re-create life there in the 1830s.

Abraham Lincoln Birthplace National Historic Site
Outside Hodgenville, Ky. (60 miles south of Louisville)

The National Park Service operates this site, which includes two locations. The Birthplace Unit near Hodgenville includes a neoclassic Memorial Building that houses a symbolic log cabin. The Boyhood Home Unit at Knob Creek, 10 miles away, includes the homestead where Lincoln spent his boyhood years until his family moved to Indiana when he was 7.

Reconstruction *New Salem, the small Illinois settlement where Lincoln spent his formative years, has been re-created as a historical tourist attraction along the lines of Williamsburg, Va. Above, visitors don 1830s-style hats to escape the summer sun*

Lincoln Boyhood National Memorial
Lincoln City, Ind. (60 miles northeast of Evansville)

The National Park Service operates this site commemorating the years Lincoln spent in Indiana, from age 7 to 22. The park includes a visitors' center; the cabin site memorial (a bronze casting of the foundation of the Lincoln cabin); a restored cabin; a historical farm; and the cemetery where Lincoln's mother is buried.

Ford's Theatre
Washington, D.C.

The restored theater reopened in 1968. Operated by the National Park Service and a private organization, the Ford's Theatre Campus includes the theater and museum, which is being renovated and will be closed until the spring of 2009.

President Lincoln's Cottage at the Soldiers' Home
Washington, D.C.

Lincoln and his family spent a quarter of his presidency at their own "Camp David," a "cottage" at the hilltop site of the Soldiers' Home in the capital, a facility for veterans. The Lincolns' 34-room country home has been restored by the National Trust for Historic Preservation, a private, nonprofit organization. Opened for public tours in 2008, it includes a visitors' center and landscaped gardens.

Lincoln Memorial
Washington, D.C.

Operated by the National Park Service and located at one end of the capital's National Mall, this beloved, moving memorial was designed by Henry Bacon. It features the famed seated statue of Lincoln by Daniel Chester French, murals by Jules Guérin and quotations by Lincoln on its walls.

Smithsonian Institution Lincoln Bicentennial Celebration
Washington, D.C.

The national museum will observe the bicentennial year of 2009 with a year-long celebration that will include displays, programs and conferences. Exhibits will be held at the Smithsonian American Art Museum, National Portrait Gallery and National Museum of American History. For more information, see *www.gosmithsonian.com/lincoln.*

Index

Index